Social M

MW01128564

Build Your Brand and Become the Best Influencer Using YouTube and Instagram Marketing! Top Personal Branding & Digital Networking Strategies

WRITTEN BY **STEPHAN ANDERSON**

Contents

Introduction

Many people have discovered creative methods to earn money using the internet. A "money-making" technique that is currently popular today is the influencer marking through personal branding on social media.

Whether you are a writer who wants to get the attention of readers from all over the world or a person with great taste in fashion and beauty, you can create your content, curate other people's great content with your flavour and make money out of it. Yes, that is possible, and this book will help you do precisely that!

On top of it, you will be able to build a sustainable business around it. You may wish to keep it small like a source of passive income, but that is your choice because people are raking in millions with just this. However, writing a book around it means that it is not as simple as it sounds. There are certain things to learn, certain things to tweak and certain hidden secrets that only the pros know. That book will tell you all that so that your start is explosive. You know how they say – well begun is half done!

But why a simple platform like Instagram and an effort-intensive platform like YouTube? You may ask that.

That is because these platforms get maximum share and engagement. That engagement quickly turns into leads and sales.

Today's Instagram influencers are not influencers by accident. It is no coincidence that some personalities have over 10, 20, 30 million followers, while other people struggle to get a few thousand. To gain a massive amount of traction on social media these days, you need a plan!

 A plan which will see your Instagram account break through the noise of a million other accounts and put you right in the influencer category which everyone is so desperate to achieve.

Top fitness Instagram influencers like Kayla Itsines, Jen Selter & Massy Arias all dominate their area's by using extremely creative Instagram tactics. Tactics which keep both new and existing followers wholly engaged in their content.

This book will give you a peek inside the world of influencers. You will learn precisely how influencers create great Instagram campaigns. That will eventually make your account stand out from the rest and get you closer to becoming a paid influencer. You could have offers coming in left right and centre for companies begging you to promote their products and services. Here is a snapshot of the highest-paid Instagram influencers earned PER POST during 2019.

Kylie Jenner - $1 Million per post

Selena Gomez - $800,000 per post

Cristiano Ronaldo - $750,00 per post

Kim Kardashian $720,00 per post

Beyoncé - $700,000 per post

Dwayne The Rock" Johnson - $650,000 per post

Justin Bieber - $650,000 per post

If each of these celebrities uploaded a sponsored Instagram post on the same day in 2019, then the bill would come to a whopping $5.27 Million! And that's just one day of the year!

Now imagine yourself as an Instagram influencer receiving just 0.1% of that revenue. Does not sound like a lot? It would be over $5,000 per post! No wonder that even the smaller Instagram influencers are earning hundreds of thousands of dollars and living a life which was entirely out of reach for them ten years ago.

There are no theories to learn from this playbook. Each section is an actionable exercise you can apply to your soon to be huge Instagram account.

Talking about YouTube, it can be seen as the heart of the social media platforms as its content is widely distributed throughout the other platforms. Four hundred tweets per minute contain a YouTube link, and YouTube's search bar is the second only after Google.

YouTube has the benefit of having one of the most engaged audiences out of the social media platforms. With tweets flooding Twitter news feeds, and posts cluttering Facebook feeds, it is harder than ever to reach followers on platforms. However, 85% of YouTube subscribers consider themselves "regular" YouTube users.

It is recommended that if you pursue a YouTube channel that you have a professional team of producers and creators as the content uploaded should maintain a high standard. However, a lot of prominent Youtubers have started with just their mobile phone and a personality. Now, video content and a strong YouTube presence can be significantly harder to establish and say Twitter, Facebook or Instagram. But if video content were right for your brand, it would be well worth the extra step.

The following sections will reveal all from exploding your following list, to engaging your followers, to creating a fantastic content strategy — all the way through to negotiating advertising deals and getting paid to post.

We will begin with the fundamentals of personal branding and why it is essential. Then, we will move to explain the basics of influencer marketing. The pointers mentioned in this chapter will help you create an attractive pitch for businesses as well. So, please read it carefully.

Next, we share the baby steps to becoming an Instagram Influencer. We take you through the entire roadmap of optimising your Instagram account for beauty, finesse and content strategy. Content creation and curation are two essential parts of any content strategy. The chapter will explain how to create a balance between the two and create a viable content plan.

The following chapter will polish your posting basics. You will learn the different formats and features of Instagram that you can make use of and how to time your posts for maximum exposure. Analytics is a crucial part of being an influencer. So, you will also get a basic understanding of the engagement rate and how you can quickly calculate it.

Every Instagram influencer is a creator, a storyteller. Therefore, it is terrific that Instagram has a story feature. You will be learning how to create super-engaging stories and give your followers a seamless experience on your Instagram profile through highlights and Instagram Live.

Finally, you will learn the best strategies to monetise your Instagram profile. Be it Affiliate Schemes, paid partnerships or collaborations, the book covers everything. Additionally, it also shares tips on how to reach out to companies to partner with you, creation of a contract, price list, etc.

Part 2 of the book is all about YouTube and becoming a YouTube celebrity. We breakdown what YouTube's algorithm is and how it favours one video over another. That chapter is significant as it covers the tactics for explosive channel growth, from the frequency of posting to YouTube SEO.

Next, you will get to understand the basics of video production and creation and how to keep coming up content for your channel. The chapter also covers simple tips and tricks to bring in traffic initially and sustainably too.

The next chapter is all about perfecting the nuances of video creation and publishing that will turn the amateur in you to a professional. Here, you will finally be the YouTube celebrity you always desired to be. The last chapter in Part 2 explores the less discussed, but smart ways to beat your competition on YouTube. Do you want to make it big on YouTube? Do not take this section lightly.

The final chapter of the book takes you back to personal branding. No matter what you do and on which platform, you are carrying your brand; and there is not enough you can do to assert it. If you do not maintain your personal brand, it will not matter how big you started or how fast you grew; you will fall.

So, take care of your personal brand. We are sending your way a bounty of luck and success.

Your personal brand

A brand is not a product or a service. It is an idea, a design, a symbol, a behaviour and a reputation. For example, both Samsung and Apple operate in the same space of technology, but they represent technology in totally different ways. That is their brand.

A brand is a distinction between what one thing is and not the other. That is what makes each one unique. In simple words, you have a few things that others have and a few things that others do not have. That is your USP and your differentiator. That will make your personal brand!

So, we all carry our personal brand. All your life, you have shared your brand with everyone you met or interacted with. How you portray yourself defines what your brand is. But do you believe that this represents you in a complete, real sense?

What is Personal Branding?

Personal branding is similar to the branding of a product or service. However, in the case of personal branding, this product or service is an individual. Politicians, actors, artists are all known for their unique tastes and style of working, which makes them resonate strongly with a particular section of folks. That is their personal brand.P

Personal Branding is a practice of marketing yourself to a specific audience of people. It is about promoting your skills, ideas & experiences to people who are interested in what you have to offer.

Let us begin with your name. That is your brand. How your appearance distinguishes you from others, is your brand design. You have different parents, values, personality, perception and qualities from others. All these make you unique.

In essence, personal branding is all about being your authentic self.

For example, you might be fantastic at putting outfits and accessories together, which people find attractive. So, with time, you gain followers on social media who appreciate your sense of styling and deem you as a style inspiration. Similarly, you might be great at online gaming, and you share tips and tricks regarding that on social media. Gradually, you gain a following of people who are interested in gaming.

Make sense?

Importance of Personal Branding

CVs or resumes are no longer enough. In future, they will exist only as fossils. What will thrive is your unique promise. Your brand. Anyone can have a similar set of skills and qualifications as yours, and so, they can poach your opportunities. To win, you need to be indispensable. You have to be not just the right fit, but the only fit for a job. Regardless of whether you wish to pursue a career or become an influencer, it would be best if you had your personal brand to sell your skills.

Here are the steps to create your personal brand:

Step 1: Know your strengths

Step 2: Know your shortcomings

Step 3: Know your values

Step 4: Identify your passion

Step 5: Find your niche

Step 6: Position yourself appropriately

Step 7: Understand your competition

Step 1: Knowing Your Strengths

Your strengths are an essential factor in creating your personal brand. It does not depend on what you think your strengths are, but on what others believe are your strong areas.

Think of people who you feel have a fabulous personal brand. You will observe that these people have complete clarity on what they want in life and who they are at their core. They know their unique selling points and what value they bring to the table. After doing the following exercise, you will join their league too. So, let us begin.

Write down the following in a notebook to identify your strengths:

1. Your career highlights
2. Professional moments or incidents that you are proud of
3. 2-3 most fulfilling projects of yours
4. Think of why you felt fulfilled while executing them or when they were done
5. The role you usually play in a group project
6. Perception of your group members about you
7. Your techniques and thought process to overcome challenges and obstacles
8. Tools that you use often
9. Professional or personal things that bring you joy, something you enjoy getting involved in
10. Things you like to discuss and debate about

Now, describe each of your strengths in just one word. Write those down too.

Pick individuals who know you, your partner, family, colleagues and friends and ask them to share their understanding of your strengths. In the wake of doing that contrast your rundowns and theirs. Show them your list and check whether they see you in the same light as you see yourself.

It might seem obvious; however, you would be astounded by the number of people who would list down all that they have ever done. Pass on your energy and connect your strengths to gauge results. Tell your target audience about your gifts. Convey it to them adequately utilising all resources accessible to you. While interacting with your audience, recall your qualities and morals. That will set you apart.

We all have certain shortcomings and acknowledging them is never easy. However, we do not wish to live a life full of disappointments. Therefore, you and we need to be honest about our shortcomings. Remember that weakness is anything from being utterly uninterested about anything in life to have limited skills to do anything of interest.

Let us do a similar activity as we did for strengths to identify your weak areas:

1. List down the things about your education and career that you do not like at all
2. Note down the reasons why you dislike those aspects
3. Think hard about your beliefs on how worthy you are and if you deserve better
4. Ask yourself if you feel drained merely by the thought of performing specific tasks
5. List down such tasks that make you feel out of action
6. Make a list of all the low points of your career
7. Write reasons against each on why you think that they were the low points
8. If you are given a group task, which role would you never like to perform, and why?
9. Have there been any tasks that you have done, but that did not bring you any joy?
10. Did these tasks fail? Why was that?
11. Do you ever give up? What makes you do that?
12. In a conversation, at what point do you feel uninspired to talk more?
13. Are there any particular topics that you feel uncomfortable talking?
14. List down 10 of your weaknesses.

Be honest with yourself. Know that there is no need to waste time on shortcomings that do not hamper your professional growth. Now, establish what limitations you can turn into strengths to kick-start your career. Start learning the skills to propel your growth. If talking to people makes you nervous, become a regular at networking events and work on yourself bit by bit.

Step 3: Knowing Your Values

Do you have some principles, a code that you use to navigate through life? Those principles form your value system. They determine your moral compass, your personality, attitude, actions, reactions, and so on. Do not confuse them with your profession.

Take five minutes to visualise these people and think what their personal brand is – what do they stand for. Understand the difference between their profession and their brand.

1. Barack Obama
2. Marie Kondo
3. Pele
4. Music band, Queen
5. Mark Manson
6. Seth Godin
7. Oprah Winfrey
8. Meryl Streep
9. Anna Winton
10. Frida Kahlo

Picture it like this: Perhaps your reason for unhappiness at work is that your work is not aligned with the values you uphold. Having values, therefore, is taking a stand for your beliefs. It is critical to align what you engage yourself in with who you are at your core.

By knowing your values, you get an understanding of who you are and what you stand for. To establish and route your thoughts in a way that matches your passion, you need to have strong values. Simply put, before involving yourself in anything, ask yourself, *"Is this in sync with my values and what I stand for?"*

Finding the values for your personal brand

1. On the internet, you can find valuable resources on how to establish your values for your brand. These may be present as lists of adjectives which you can use to describe your values.

2. Pick out a list that you find suitable for yourself and by process of elimination, choose the top five words that make sense to your understanding of yourself.

3. Now, think why you chose those words specifically and define what they mean to you.

4. Use them to build your mission statement and hold yourself accountable if you are not respecting your values.

5. Communicate these values everywhere – in your CV, website, social media platforms and blog posts.

Step 4: Identifying Your Passion

Have a passion for what you do! That is the biggest secret. It might seem difficult to reconcile the idea of passion and work. But it is not impossible. Clubbing your passion and work will bring you more joy than you can ever imagine. It will keep you inspired and wanting more. That is why influencers are flourishing. They did not take the beaten path or picked a career because many people were making easy money out of it. They picked it because they felt passionate about it and turned it into a viable business model. With passion, you can do that too!

If you still cannot put the finger on your passion, recall a time when you found it challenging to wait to do something. Rewind to the day when you jumped out of your bed in the morning. Think of the things that broke you into tears of joy. Do not forget the projects that unleashed your creativity and filled your head with ideas. See, it is all about feeling stimulated and motivated to do something. That something is your passion!

Ask yourself:

1. What do I like about my current job?
2. If I were to volunteer, which charity would you choose? Why?
3. How do most of your days go and in doing what?

Now take a minute to think about the potential influencers you follow on Instagram. As you do that, answer the following questions in your head:

- What do I love about my current job?
- Which would the charity of my choice if I were to volunteer in future? Why?
- What do I spend most of my time doing?

The chances are you follow certain influencers because they create valuable content in your areas of interest. These areas of interest are also called "niches".

Step 5: Finding Your Niche

The following exercise will help you understand more about what your niche could be and how you can start to build the foundations of your personal brand. Be as specific as you can when answering the questions below. You will need this information later down the line.

1. Who are you? (Write a short paragraph.)
2. What makes you unique?
3. List all of your passions (Don't just list things you are "kind of interested in", but the things you are genuinely passionate about.)
4. What are you good at? (The skills that distinguish you from your friends and family? It can be anything. It might help to think about what people compliment you on and what do you get attention for)
5. Based on the above information, who could your audience be? (To make it easier, make a list starting with "people who are interested in".

Now you have a list of "niches" that you could become a mega influencer in before we get into the techniques needed to grow a huge following.

Step 6: Positioning Yourself

Once you are crystal clear about your values, strengths, attributes, niche, and passion, it is time to now position yourself. What does that mean exactly? It means that you establish how you would like others to see you based on your qualities, strengths, values, attributes, and passion. Do not forget – it is all about authenticity. No matter where you work, you must be consistent about who you say you are.

So, create a positioning statement for yourself. Pin it on a board. You can use this statement during interviews too. It is not going to be about a boring career summary, but a powerful and fresh take on where you see yourself. It will capture your essence and uniqueness.

Step 7: Understanding your competition

Make a list of ten mega influencers in any particular niche or industry. Take a look at how they present their accounts and the kind of content they are posting. What times are they posting? How many times do they update their content? How are they interacting with their followers? How many social media platforms are they present? Is there content same everywhere or are they creating and posting different content everywhere? If yes, what are the key differences, and how do they help these influencers?

Do not try to memorise it. Chart it. Yes, create a chart of influencers who you envy or find irresistible. Use the following pointers to fill in the chart against the name of each. Do not slack here as the chart you create now will come in handy when you create a killer content campaign for your brand.

1. Account Name: Are the account name and handle different?
2. Niche: Do they operate in multiple niches? What is the ratio?
3. Display Picture: Is it a logo or a picture? Is it generic or a decent shot?

4. Bio: Add a summary of what the account bio states.

5. Call to Action (or CTA for short): Simply put, does the bio direct followers to do something specific? For example, does it ask them to click follow? Visit a website?

6. Content-Type: Does the account have videos, images or both? What does the account have more of?

7. The theme of the content: What kind of images/videos is the account sharing with its followers? Is it short "humour" videos? Amazing landscape images? Selfies of the account owner? Product images?

8. Followers: How many followers does the account have? How many are they following?

9. Engagement: Engagement means the number of likes, views, and comments each post is receiving. Look at the last 3 - 5 posts on each account and note these down. The more likes and comments show what your audience is reacting strongly to.

10. Posting schedule: How often is the account posting? Is it once per day? Three times per day? 6 times per day?

Seeing what successful accounts are doing is one of the most effective ways to grow your personal brand account.

Influencer marketing: Understanding the Basics

Whenever a celebrity does something, it creates buzz and turns into a piece of breaking news or a topic of gossip. When a similar thing happens in business, it becomes a 'hot issue'. There are many ways companies create such hot issues, and one of them is using "Influencer Marketing".

The current day and age are filled with marketing messages and business slogans. Think of an advertisement. What came to your mind? Magazine headlines? Or TV Commercials?

In influencer marketing, it is more straightforward and more accessible. The influencer will say a few magical sentences on a short video and Voila! Sales start pouring in! These influencers with their vast and huge following can make businesses stand out from chaotic and old-school advertising techniques out there. Additionally, they will also bring massive value to your brand.

So, what is Influencer Marketing?

Before we dig deep into its understanding and insights. We first define the two words:

Influence is the ability to affect the behaviour, development, decisions and character of someone, and even the impact itself.

Marketing is a way with which businesses promote or sell their products and services.

So, when combined, Influencer Marketing becomes a kind of marketing that utilises "influencers" who can influence others to buy what are they promoting or selling.

Even though Influencer marketing seems like a hot issue currently, it is nothing new. In fact, influencer marketing was born at the same time as the discovery of social media sites happened. Celebrities, Sports Enthusiast, and Thought Leaders were the first influencers of their niches and brands partnered with them to promote and sell their products and services.

So, here, we share a few characteristics of influencer marketing that make it so compelling and relevant:

Influencer Marketing is Unique

Social media communication has already allowed everyone to voice out their opinions. Anyone who can speak properly and has an internet connection is welcome to create and share their content. Any smartphone user is capable of producing high-quality photographs and sharing them with the world through their social media account. Those who have the great and highest engagement will rise in status and stands a chance to become an influencer for that particular niche.

Influencer Marketing is Authentic

Indeed, it is. You must have seen those advertisement online that claim to know the easiest way to lose belly fat. Do you think those things work? Did those advertisements ever convince you that those claims might be right? Or, how about soap advertisements that promise to remove all tan or freckles in just one wash? Is that even remotely possible?

Such advertisements that are full of fake promises are what give Influencer Marketing its authenticity and efficacy.

Influencer campaigns are organic and genuine than those advertisements that are scripted. Why? First, Influencers rise from the general population. In a way, they are people's champions. They are visible and had already used the product or service they are promoting. They are those role models and leaders who have gone through strict public scrutiny to build that level of trust and credibility. Therefore, invest your time, effort and money on leveraging their audience and connecting with them as you will witness much better results and ROI.

Influencers Help You with Your Brand Image

Social media can drive traffic to your business website. It can strengthen your bond with your customers, boost your overall SEO and generate organic media coverage. Influencers emerge as your "Superman" when you need a hand to increase your brand's recall and create a buzz about something on social media. Influencers will help you target the appropriate demographic, grow your network online, share ideas on how to create content for your business that and bolsters your SEO.

Influencer Marketing Is Cost-Effective

If you are tired from posting flyers everywhere that did not bring you any sales, try influencer marketing. It may turn out to be the best method for your business.

There is no fixed price for Influencer Marketing. You can either offer them a free item, pay them based on their performance, or discuss a flat rate for their services. Nonetheless, you will observe that influencer marketing will give you the best ROI. Plenty of research has proved that it is more affordable and effective than any other form of traditional advertising.

Influencer Marketing is nothing like celebrity endorsements or paid gambling. It is about being authentic and unique and leveraging the genuine relationship between the brand, influencer, and their audience. That is precisely what distinguished influencer marketing from other marketing strategies.

Social Media Influencers: A Skin-Deep Industry?

While one spends hours scrolling through social media and admiring the picture-perfect luxurious life of influencers, one is bound to think that an attractive face and some luck are all it takes to become one of them. The reality, however, is often a lot different from such wishful imaginations.

So, here are the three fundamental traits of a successful social media influencer of today:

Identity

To move beyond being a forgettable pleasant face on Instagram, you need to establish a distinctive digital personality. That will require you to have a clear roadmap of content creation and how you aim to develop a reputation for being a go-to person for any particular niche.

An authentic influencer is also known to create buzz on their own and not merely ride on the trends with generic content. That means maintaining an intricate balance between the current market trends and being your avant-garde self.

Likability

Apart from looking pleasant and being creative, it is essential to have an amicable personality. When it comes to monetising the influence, influencers need to establish a healthy working relationship with brands and businesses. With the mushrooming of micro-influencers, it is a buyer's market.

So, when two influencers share the same niche, audience and almost identical influence, businesses and agencies will gravitate towards those who easier to work with than the over-the-top divas. It is common-sense to have common courtesy, especially when an influencer's critical criteria are to be likeable.

Integrity

While it is crucial to pay your bills even as a social media influencer which means business, one must not forget about integrity. It has to be your constant guiding principle. That means that the influencers must genuinely prefer a brand and its offerings to be able to 'sell' it and persuade their followers to 'buy' the content and to buy the product in question. A mismatch of influencer and brand will at best make little sales and at worst, tarnish the reputation of the influencer

Using significant persuasiveness in their niches, influencers may monetise the influence, use it to further causes that are close to their hearts or stay as an entertainer. To be able to choose these options, an individual must meet among the necessary prerequisites. While a pleasing appearance does help initially, authentic influencers are more than genetics and make-up.

Influencer marketing can be considered as an effective strategy to attract and engage with the potential and existing customers.

You can no longer question the significance of social marketing. Everyone is using the social marketing agency or channels for personal and professional purposes. These days, most businesses are leveraging the benefits of social media networks to expand their influence and distinguish themselves from the competition. They want to go beyond just maintaining an online presence. So, they need to stretch out their brick-and-mortar retail to digital, and here, they must take advantage of influencers and technology.

The ascent of social media has reignited enthusiasm for influencer marketing. In today's digital times, persuading the audience towards purchase is not limited to actors and celebrities. Any well-known blogger or a social media influencer can make that happen. Anyone who has established his or her credibility with a broad audience and has a considerable following online is an influencer. Their reliability, skill, and realness can convince consumers to draw in with your image. What is more, that is the reason it is recommended to set up a potential association with them and arrange your advertising exercises around them.

Becoming an Instagram influencer is not a sprint. It is a marathon. Growing a highly engaged following will take time but will profit you massively in the long run. Companies are competing harder than ever to seek out and partner with social media influencers. They want influencers who have excellent engagement rates and a loyal following. A good Instagram Influencer is bombarded with partnership offerings from all around the world. Let us make it happen for you!

Who is an Instagram Influencer?

An appropriate definition of an "Instagram Influencer" would be a user who has established credibility with an audience, who can persuade others by virtue of their trustworthiness and authenticity to act.

This definition tells us that an influencer is:

- someone with a massive network of followers
- whose followers share the interests of this influencer
- someone who is known to be an honest person and people's champion

Honest is the keyword here. The reason is that no company wants to be associated with dishonest people. By using this trust, your influence, they can (and will) persuade followers to buy and use the different products and services you promote (which are theirs).

In return for your influence, businesses will pay you to put their products or services in front of your followers. This, in turn, gives them the exposure they need to sell more goods. That is a form of monetisation which we will discuss shortly.

So, as an Instagram influencer, you have a responsibility, to be honest, and only promote products you believe in. If you choose to use your influence to encourage hate or negativity, then you can kiss your chances of monetising your Instagram goodbye!

When are you officially an influencer?

Technically you are an influencer the minute someone acts on the back of your recommendation. Whether an audience member buys a product you have talked about, visited a restaurant you recommended or watched a movie you raved about. The real question is, what do companies and brands look for when seeking to partner up with Instagram influencers.

Understand that all businesses and brands are different, and when it comes to partnering with influencers. They will look for entirely different characteristics, attributes and metrics. Whether it be the niche you are in, the content you have posted or your image. They all have different requirements.

With that said, most companies generally look for the same two fundamental things before they look for anything else. These are:

1. A large follower base (usually a minimum of 10,000)
2. A high engagement rate over your last ten posts (+3% minimum)

These are general guidelines. Some smaller business will be happy to partner with you if you only have 3,000 followers and a 10% engagement rate; whereas others will want influencers with over a million followers and a 1.5% engagement rate.

Again, these two points are only the beginning. Companies may then look at your content, your image, your niche, how you behave with your followers, your captions etc. Everything in this playbook works coordinated with each other and has been laid out to help you build the best Instagram account and maximise your chances in creating business deals with potential partners.

Optimising a Beautiful Instagram Account

This chapter will tell you how to create an Instagram profile which sticks out from the rest and gives you the best chances of ranking highest in the search results. Before we work through each section and maximise your Instagram account. You will need to get familiar with each part of your Instagram and understand its purpose and why it is essential.

Instagram Username or Handle

Now you will need your smartphone or device and your influencer study chart at the ready while you work through each section.

Your Instagram Username or Handle is the name which displays at the top of your Instagram page. That @handle is the first thing which makes your account stand out. It is your unique ID which everyone on Instagram will know you by. Here is some information that you should know about this @handle:

1. Only you will have the @handle you choose, no one else on Instagram will have the same @handle.
2. It will appear in the Instagram search results when people search for you or accounts similar to yours.
3. People see the @handle when you like or comment on images or videos across Instagram

To keep it easy for your audience, have a handle that is short, nice and convenient to remember. You might find that the name you wanted is not available because an account already exists by that name. In such a case, do not start adding random numbers to your handle name.

First, try some variations with dots and underscores. If that does not work, try adding words like official, yours, I am, etc. or your niche or country. Add numbers only when you have exhausted all these options and even then, use a number that is relevant to your personal brand.

To change your @handle, open up your Instagram app on your smartphone or device and head to your profile page. Click edit profile" and update the "username" section. Instagram does an excellent job of letting you know if a username is already taken so play around with it and create a username which sticks out to your new and existing followers.

Your Instagram Name

The name section of Instagram differs from the @handle we discussed in the previous part.

That gives visitors a bit of extra information on who you are and what your name is. For your personal branded account, we suggest you use your name or your name plus the niche you are in. Your name will appear in bold right underneath your profile picture (which we will discuss in the next section) so visitors' eyes will be drawn directly to it each time they visit your profile.

Again, you may already have your Instagram name setup in a way which quickly identifies who you are if that is the case, fantastic! You can move to the next section. To update your name, click "edit profile" then update the "name" section.

The critical thing to remember about the name section is that Instagram search function will use it to find you when people start to look you up.

Choosing the Perfect Instagram Display Picture

Before we look at how to update your Instagram display picture, let us look at the top 5 things which make the perfect Instagram display picture.

1. **Make your display picture all about your brand:**
   Remember your brand is you! So, create a good display image all about you. An excellent clear headshot makes the perfect display image. Why? Because you are selling you! You are the brand; you are the influencer, you are the owner of this account, so make it clear to your followers what your account is all about.

2. **Think about the background of your display image:**

When selecting a headshot for your Instagram display image, the environment is significant. It does not just add to the look and feel of your display image, but the entire appearance of your account. A carefully selected background, which matches the overall colour palette of your account, will look super professional and impressive.

3. **Keep your display picture up to date:**

   You want people to know that you are fully active on Instagram. It does not look great if it is summertime and your display image is of you on a skiing vacation. Try to keep your display image up to date as possible. If you choose a seasonal theme for your display image, then remember to update it when that particular season ends. Again, you do not want as Christmassy display image in February!

   Choosing a neutral theme means your display images can be used for longer but not too long. It is good to update your image everyone 6 - 8 weeks as it keeps it fresh and get your followers interested enough to visit your profile when they see it change.

4. **Consider using props in your display image:**

   Is your niche makeup? Then make your picture look like you are about to apply makeup. Is your niche fitness? Then hold a dumbbell in your display image. Your image needs to capture you, your amazing personality and your niche all at the same time. If this seems a tad tricky, then at least get yourself a beautiful and exciting background.

5. **Choose the right image size:**

   The size of your profile image is significant. Instagram displays your profile image at a size of 110 x 110 pixels. So, when you are viewing an Instagram profile on your smartphone or tablet. You will see the profile image in the size of 110 by 110 pixels. It has not very big, but big enough that you can get an indication of what the picture is about. To get the most precise display image, we suggest you upload a display image which is a little bit bigger at around 500x500 pixels.

   The reason for this is because:

- This particular image size will display the most precise image, making you even more recognisable. Especially when people visit your profile and see your image in the search field and comments section.
- The image size keeps the vital image square. Instagram loves square images because it then crops your image into a circle of 110 by 110 pixels.

You can adjust and move your image before you upload it to your profile. When you do this, make sure your image is centred and looking symmetrical.

Most pictures you take on your Smartphone will be a good enough size to upload. There will be further information in later sections on how to create the perfect image size using tools such as Canva.

Creating an Instagram Bio That Sticks Out

You will find your Instagram bio sitting underneath your name, and it instantly tells users briefly about who you are. A good bio can capture visitors' attention and entice them to follow you.

As an influencer, you want your bio to sell your Instagram account and nothing else. You want to get people to hit that follow button, so they see all of your regular updates. You could take an influential approach or a funny one. It does not matter; the important thing is that people connect with immediately.

Some research suggests that you have less than 2 seconds to make an impression on Instagram. That means that as soon as someone clicks on your profile, they will click off it almost instantly if nothing immediately grabs their attention. As an influencer, you want your bio to grab the reader's attention, connect with them in some way and then direct them to take a specific action. In this case, you want them to click "follow".

Some do's and don'ts of Instagram bios

Emojis

Emojis are an excellent tool for engaging visitors. They make your bio look colourful and will break up the text nicely. However, do not overuse them as it will make your bio look cluttered. Just a few scattered throughout will be enough to make your bio look fresh and exciting.

Also, try to add in emojis which are relevant to what you are communicating. If you want to add in your bio that you are a dog lover, then use a dog emoji. If you are adding to your bio that you love make-up, then add a lipstick emoji. If you use emojis which are not congruent with what you are saying, then it could look confusing and cost you followers.

Format

You want your bio to be aesthetically pleasing and easy on the eye. The way you do this is by making sure the spacing is right. Take a look at the profiles on your chart and see how their bios are spaced.

The Instagram app is coded in such a way that it does not recognises spaces in the bio. It does not accept new lines which makes your bio look clunky and crowded. The best way to create your bio is in the notes app on your Smartphone or device. Then copy and paste directly into the bio section of the edit screen. That will give you a nicely formatted bio which will grab the attention of any new visitors and improve your chances of converting them into a new follower.

Your Call to Action (CTA)

You have probably seen the phrase "call to action" a couple of times so far. But what does it mean? A call to action is a short phrase, like Book Now or Click Here, which instructs a visitor to take a particular action. Have you ever seen a website which asks you to "buy now" or watched a YouTube video which asks you to "hit the subscribe button"? That is a call to action! So, what is your call to action?

That is all about making you an influencer on Instagram, and what do all Instagram influencers have lots of? Followers!!! That is right; you want followers. You want people who visit your profile to hit the follow button and become a new follower.

When you update your bio always make sure the last line of text has a "call to action". Some good examples you can use are Follow Me, Hit the Follow Button NOW, Click Follow NOW for Loads of Amazing Updates, Tap Follow to See More of Me, Click Follow & Send Me a Message.

Use emojis around your call to action, so it draws the visitor's eyes to it. A right call to action could be the difference between someone clicking off your profile and clicking follow.

Do not forget to experiment with your call to action; you may find some "call to actions" work better than others depending on who your audience is.

Creating the Ultimate Content Strategy

"Good content isn't about storytelling; it's about telling your story well."

There are nine types of content you can choose from when posting on Instagram. These categories will give you countless ideas on what to post to your account. The important thing is that you are posting and getting your personal brand out there and in front of people. The nine categories are:

1. The Selfie
2. What's Happening
3. Quotes
4. Humour
5. Short Videos
6. Trending Daily Hashtags
7. Behind the Scenes
8. Products in Use
9. The How-to Post

Let us look at each category in more detail.

#1: The Selfie

As an influencer, people need to see you, and they need to see who they are interacting with. So, post selfies of yourself wherever you go. Remember, that backgrounds are just as crucial with selfies so get creative.

#2: What's happening?

What are you up to? Are you out shopping and find a costly pair of shoes? Post it! Come across a fantastic statue or piece of the street? Post it! Are you just sat on the grass reading a book? Post it!

What is happening posts are not only excellent opportunities for posting exciting things, but they can turn into unique selfie opportunities too.

#3: Quotes

Posting your favourite quotes is a perfect way to engage with your followers. Quotes can be funny, serious, informative, intelligent, and people react to them well.

#4: Humour

Anything you find funny should be posted on Instagram. People love to laugh, and if they laugh at something you have posted, then they will connect with your account in an extremely positive way. Do not forget to keep it tidy and try not to post anything which makes you look like a clown.

#5: Short Videos

Instagram lets you post short videos up to 60 seconds long. Short videos are just an alternative to images so you can post selfie videos, what are you up to videos, Trending Daily Hashtag Videos, Product in Use Videos and Funny Videos. Video is becoming more and more popular, so do not be shy! Post videos as often as you can.

#6: Trending Daily Hashtags

Each day Instagram has some top trending hashtags which you should use to get maximum exposure. For example, Monday has #MondayMotivation, Tuesday has #TipTuesday, Wednesday has #Workout Wednesday and so on. We will discuss more hashtags in the next sections.

#7: Behind the Scenes

Behind the scenes posts are usually created by companies who want to show you their business "behind the scenes". It helps followers understand the who is who of their industry. For influencers, behind the scenes could be a look at their home life, pictures of their pets, their homes, their families etc.

#8: Products in Use

As an influencer, you may get asked to promote products or services. An excellent method is to post the "product in use" image. Whether it is eyeliner or a protein bar the beauty of the product in use shot is that it helps your followers envisage what it is like using the product themselves. That pleases companies who may sponsor you to promote more of their product.

#9: The How-to Post

This type of post does wonders for engagement because it gives the user free knowledge that they did not have access to before. Although not impossible, you can create a good "how-to" post using just one image but do not forget you can add up to 10 images in one post using the carousel option or post a 1-minute long video. Choose whichever feels right for you!

Curating Other People's Content

When you browse Instagram (or the web in general), you may come across a piece of content that you like so much that you want to repost it. Although you can do this, you need to know that posting copyrighted content without permission could be a violation of the law.

Here are some things to consider when reposting other people's content:

1. Where possible, get permission from the content owner to repost. Otherwise, mention the name of the original creator to give due credit. There are lots of cool apps on the app store designed to make reposting easy. These apps automatically credit the creator, so you do not need to.

2. Many websites offer royalty-free images. You can take pictures from there and use them in your content.
3. Two other great sources for content are Reddit and Tumblr. People from all around the world post content they find interesting specific to certain topics. You can use that content to share on your feed.

By using the above categories, you will never run out of things to post. Do not set yourself any limits; just let the content flow freely and see what people react to. You will find that some posts do well, and others do not. Pay attention to what posts are getting the most likes and comments. As time goes on, you will be able to see what your followers like, which means you can post more of it.

Instagram Posting: The Basics

As an Instagram user, you will know how to post basic images at the very least. The following information walks you through some of the additional features Instagram has to liven up your content. You must mix up the use of these features to keep your content fresh and engaging.

In-built Instagram Tools for Posting

Boomerang

It is a free app by Instagram, which is also in-built in its UI. It takes a burst of photographs and loops them backwards and forwards into a "boomerang" video. It brings images to life and gives them an excellent 3D feel. Give it a go!

Layout

The Layout is another app created by Instagram, which lets you create funky collage images. That is great for your content strategy because it gives you more variety in your posts. Download it now and play around with it.

Select Multiple or Carousel

The select-multiple tool is another feature inside Instagram, which allows you to create a carousel of images. You can select up to 10 images in 1 post which your followers can swipe through. It is another cool feature which again gives you more variety in your content creation

All of the above apps are accessible when you click the "upload" button located in the centre of your Instagram profile home screen.

Post Captions

Adding captions to posts is one of the most underestimated features of Instagram. The word caption comes from the old French word "caption" which means "capture". And that should tell you the function of your captions. They should be capturing your follower's attention and grabbing hold of it.

A great caption will amplify the engagement of your post and boost your exposure to more followers across the Instagram platform. That is a skill all good influencers have!

Instagram captions allow you to add up to 2200 characters, including emoji. So, you have quite a big space to say what you want to say. That does not mean you have to max out the character count each time you post in fact, quite the opposite. When it comes to captions, less is more!

Now here are the top 6 things you need to consider when creating a high-quality caption:

1. Make the first line attention-grabbing.
   Remember, that Instagram allows only the first few lines, usually140 characters, of your caption openly and rest everything is tucked under 'Read More'. To read any more than that, the viewer will need to click the "more" button that appears in your caption. So, you need to make the first line of your caption stand out and grab the viewer's attention to the point they have to click more and read the rest.

2. Ask a question.
   It is a smart way to interact with your audience. Asking questions and encouraging people to answer can open up a massive conversation with your followers and potential new followers. Get people to come forward with their own opinions and experiences. Do not forget to respond to the best comments. People are delighted to see someone they admire to engage with them. That is an excellent step to creating a solid fan base.

3. Direct people to your bio.
   Adding your own Instagram handle into your caption is a powerful way to get people to visit your bio. You can create a caption telling people about the content in your profile.

4. Call to action.
   Create a caption which directs the viewers to take a specific action. This could be to "Tag A Friend Who Likes Coffee" or "Visit My Profile to Find Out More.

5. Format your caption.

   Just like the bio, Instagram is not great when it comes to formatting your captions. An excellent app to download is "Caption Writer". That great little tool is easy to use and completely free! Just type your caption in the format you want then copy and paste it over to Instagram.

6. Change up your fonts.

   Yes, you can choose different fonts for your Instagram captions. An excellent place to get cool fonts is www.igfonts.io or www.instgramfonts.com. Check each site out!

More Amazing Tools for Creating Amazing Content

Canva.com

Canva is a cool, free, graphics design site. It is simple to use and has lots of fantastic stuff which will help you create some eye-catching content.

Canva uses drag-and-drop features, so you do not need any experience in design. There are loads of templates you can use for Instagram posts and Instagram Stories too.

Adobe Spark Post & Adobe Spark Video

These two apps can help you create some stunning content for your Instagram page. They do take a bit more getting used to than Canva, but when used correctly, it can make your content stand out.

Both Adobe Spark Post & Video are available in the app store.

Adobe Photoshop

The adobe photoshop app is a professional image editing tool you can download for free. With this app, you can touch up your photos, remove blemishes, add text and change perspectives. It is awesome!

Adobe Photoshop has some cool paid features that you can make use of. However, the free version offers you more than you can get anywhere else.

When to post your content could be the difference between 100 likes and 1000 likes. The right time for your post to go up depends on the content your posting, your follower count, your hashtag strategy and your location on the globe.

Your account is unique, and your best time to post will be too. Data suggests that Wednesdays tend to generate more likes per post on average. However, it is only a tiny bit higher than any other day during the week. With that in mind, do not worry too much about what day of the week to post.

What you should worry about is the best time to post. Again, the data shows that the average number of likes is low during the early hours of the morning. They then start to pick up as we move towards the time when most people are waking up from their sleep and are just beginning their day.

There is a point during midday and early evening when activity is the highest. Some analysis says that Instagram gets busy during lunch periods and when people come home from work or school etc. With that information, make a note of these times and consider them when you are posting.

One great tool to use is an app called "When to Post" which is available for free in the app store. That amazing app will monitor your account and give you the three best times to post every day.

Frequency of Posting

There is no specific number of posts you should create each day to get your account out there. It differs for every account right across Instagram. So, focus more on the quality of the post rather than the quantity. However, as a general advice post a minimum of once per week and not more than thrice in one day.

This balance is vital to show your followers that you are active but not addicted. What is the point of uploading ten posts in one day, which are of average quality that make you look like a spam account?

Choose quality over quantity.

Instagram Engagement Rate

Engagement rate is something that the Instagram algorithm monitors regularly. It is a way of determining how effective a piece of content is with its audience.

The reason Instagram works out the engagement rate is that it wants to make sure its users only see the best content on its platform. For example, if you follow #adorabledogs, then Instagram wants to make sure you only see good, quality content relating to "adorable dogs". It will do this by searching its platform for any content with the "adorable dogs" hashtag. Content will then be prioritised based on the highest engagement rate.

Instagram does this to remain competitive. If they did not, then it would be full of trash content that people would not be interested in. That could result in people leaving the platform for a competitor.

Instagram automatically applies a simple algorithm to each post to calculate its engagement rate.

Calculation of Engagement Rate

Engagement rate (ER) is worked out like this:

(Number of likes + Number of comments)/ (Number of followers) x 100 = ER%

For instance, after posting a picture, you get 500 likes, 40 comments, and you have 4500 followers. The math would look like this:

500 (likes) + 40 (comments) / 4500 (followers) x 100 = 12% (ER%)

So, this post would have a 12% engagement rate which is absolutely massive. The average Instagram account has a 3% engagement rate. Anything consistently above

3%, mixed in with a high number of followers, and you are considered an Instagram Influencer.

If your math is not high then no problem, there is a simple calculator you can use to work out your engagement rate for each post. Just fill in the blanks and let the calculator work it out for you.

www.iginfluencerplaybook.com/Instagram-engagement-rate-calculator

Before we proceed to the next section, here is one thing to note: Although working out your engagement rate is a good thing; you want to focus most of your time on your content itself. Combining that with the strategies you are about to learn in the next section will naturally skyrocket your engagement rate bringing in a massive wave of new followers.

Maxing Out Your Engagement Rate

Now you know about engagement rate, let us look at the strategies which will get your content in front of millions of users across the world. We will go over the three most effective ways to boost your posts and get the maximum engagement rate. These are:

- Hashtags
- Geotags
- Social Proof

Hashtags

Hashtags are short descriptive pieces of text which categorise your content and make it easily searchable. So, let us say that you want to search for Gucci. You could type in "Gucci" in the search function, and it will bring back all the available images which have #Gucci in the caption or the comments section of the post.

People generally follow the hashtag they are interested in too. So, someone who follows "#Gucci" will often see Gucci content in their feeds. Before we find and create some fantastic hashtags for your account, take a look at some of the dos and don'ts of posting content using hashtags.

1. Keep your hashtags 30 or less in one post.

   Each post allows to use up to 30 hashtags in total so use them all! The more hashtags you use, the more people will see your content. The more people see your content, the more followers you get. If you try to use more than 30 hashtags, Instagram will not let you upload your post.

2. Keep your hashtags relevant.

   If you are making a post about working out in the gym, then you will want to use tags such as #fitness #gym #workout etc. You would not use hashtags like #catsofinstagram or #makeupartist because it would look confusing to anyone viewing your content. Keep your hashtags relevant to you, your post and your personal brand.

3. Insert hashtag in the comments section of each post.

   You can insert your hashtags in either the caption section or the comments section of your post. It is recommended that you post your hashtags in the comments section. The reason for this is that it keeps your captions looking clean for each post, so users will not initially see what hashtags you have used. Once you have submitted your content along with the caption, revisit the post and click the speech bubble icon to open the comment box. Here you can add the hashtags relevant to your post.

4. Try to mix up your hashtags.

   Some people save their favourite hashtags and copy them each time they post. There is some evidence to suggest that Instagram considers the use of the same hashtags over and over again as spam. That would be a disaster because you could end up having your account banned. Avoid being repetitive and mix your hashtags up. You will get maximum exposure this

5. There are specific hashtags you must avoid.

   Avoid any hashtags which are asking for follows such as #follow4follow, #pleasefollow, #followme, #like4follow etc. Potentially using these tags could get your account banned, which is the last thing you want as an Instagram influencer. Also, you do not want to come across as desperate for followers.

The best part of hashtags is that you can literally hashtag anything! You can use existing hashtags, or you can even make them up. The idea is to use hashtags which are being used more frequently because this increases your exposure to more potential followers.

A great tool to find top trending hashtags is www.tagsforlikes.com which monitors Instagram each day for the top trending hashtags. You can use these hashtags to build your following and personal brand. The great thing about www.tagsforlikes.com is that it gives top trending hashtags for different categories too. If you are having coffee with friends, then tagsforlikes can provide you with the top trending coffee & friends hashtags etc.

When you are adding hashtags, think about what you are doing, who you are with, what your post is about, and where you are. You can even hashtag the city or country you are in!

The point is you need to hashtag everything relevant at that moment in time! Do not hold back, go wild; this can be the difference between 5 likes and 5000 likes.

Daily Trending Hashtags

There is a tradition on Instagram, which means you will see specific hashtags pop up on certain days of the week. That is 100% something you need to take advantage of because so many Instagram users subscribe to these hashtags.

Below is a list of the top 79 hashtags which trend Monday through to Sunday. These hashtags are a great way to get exposure as well as giving you some inspiration on what to post. Keep this list handy and try to incorporate them on the days you post.

Monday

#MondayMotivation #MotivationMonday #MondayBlues #MarketingMonday #MusicMonday #MeatlessMonday #MaxoutMonday #MondayRun #MondayOutfit

#MindfulMonday #ManicureMonday #MancrushMonday (or #MCM) #MondayFunday #ManicMonday

Tuesday

#TravelTuesday #TransformationTuesday #TipTuesday #TechTuesday #TuesdayTasting #TuesdayShoesday #GoodNewsTues #TuesdayTunes #TakeMeBackTuesday #TastyTuesday

Wednesday

#WomancrushWednesday (or #WCW) #Humpday #WorkoutWednesday #WisdomWednesday #WellnessWednesday #WayBackWednesday #WoofWednesday #Winesday #WineWednesday #WackyWednesday #WomenWednesday #WinItWednesday

Thursday

#ThrowbackThursday (or #TBT) #ThankfulThursday #Thursdate #ThirstyThursday #ThoughtfulThursday #ThursdayThoughts #TGIT (Thank God It is Thursday)

Friday

#FlashBackFriday #FearlessFriday #FashionFriday #FictionFriday #FridayReads #FollowFriday (or #FF) #FeatureFriday #FitnessFriday #FridayFun #FridayNight #FactFriday #FreebieFriday #TGIF (Thank God It is Friday)

Saturday

#Caturday #SaturdayStyle #SaturdaySweat #SaturdaySpecial #SaturdaySale #SaturdayNight #SaturdayNightFever #SaturdayShoutOut (or #SS)

Sunday

#SundayFunday #SundayRead #SpotlightSunday #StartupSunday #SundaySweat #SelfieSunday #WeekendVibes #ScienceSunday #SundayBrunch

A geotag is another great way to get exposure from users in specific towns or cities. Instagram uses your physical location to tag your content to whichever location you choose.

For example, if you tag your post to Los Angeles, California, then people following or located in LA will have a higher chance of seeing your content. Tagging a location is easy. Simply use the "Add Location" option when uploading a post and choose a location. It does not have to be your hometown, either!

The good thing about geotags is that it is not just limited to towns or cities. You can geotag in venues, bars, clubs and shopping malls. Any location on the map will be available to geotag!

Social Proof

Social proof is a potent tool when it comes to increasing your engagement rate. But what is it?

Social proof comes in many forms both online and offline, but it boils down to this. People love what is widespread, and the more popular something is, the more exciting and trustworthy it becomes. It is a form of human psychology.

Have you bought something from Amazon and observed the star rating? You probably did not buy an item which only had a 1-star rating. Instead, you went for the 5-star rating. Even if it costs a little more, that is social proof.

So how does social proof work on Instagram?

Research has shown that you are more likely to engage with a piece of content if it has a higher amount of likes and comments. People follow the social norm, so the more likes and comments you see on a piece of content. The more exciting, trustworthy and valuable the content is perceived to be. So how do you max out your social proof?

You are about to learn the top 3 ways you can max out your social proof. These strategies have helped some of the biggest influencers on the Instagram kick start their careers as a social media influencer so take them seriously.

Note that these methods are only used to gain traction in your following and not something to be used long term. When your account eventually reaches the 10k followers' mark, and your engagement is above the standard 3%. Your social proof is something which will increase each time you post.

Here are the top 3 strategies to kickstart your social proof on Instagram.

1. **Tell your current following when you post.**

   How do you do that? Simple! You do it through your Instagram story, which we will go through in the next section. (This is powerful)

2. **Add a call to action (CTA) on your post.**

   We discussed the call to action in the first part of the playbook. When you create a post, you should add a phrase in the first line of the caption which invites the user to like and/or comment on your post.

   For example, let us say you upload a post of that delicious Strawberry Frappuccino you have just bought at Starbucks. The first line of the caption could read "Like if you love Frappes!" or "What's your favourite Frappe? Comment Below!!".

   Research has shown that by adding a call to action to your posts. You can increase likes and comments by up to 250%!

3. **Power Likes**

   Power likes is a system provided by the super successful social media management company GoSo. They manage thousands of genuine, high-quality accounts across Instagram. For approximately $35.00, GoSo will deliver 100 natural likes to two of your posts each day for a full month. That massively boosts your engagement rate and social proof at the same time. Sign up today and give it a try, once you provide your Instagram @handle and place your order. The likes start rolling in after around 15 minutes.

   That is a great way to boost your engagement rate instantly. As your likes start to flow through, your post will rank higher in users Instagram feed, meaning even more organic likes and follows.

Instagram story feature is quite possibly the most engaging and accessible form of social media at this moment in time. In fact, as of 2019, Instagram has over 1.5 billion users worldwide. Over 60% of which view and create Instagram stories almost daily. That is over 750 million people worldwide viewing and posting content!

That is a lot of people!

So, the question is, how can you make your Instagram stories stand out above the rest of the crowd?

In this chapter, you will learn,

- What Instagram stories are and why they are so important.
- The Do's and Don'ts of Instagram Stories
- What to post on Instagram Stories?
- Top 10 tips for creating super-engaging stories
- Story Highlights tactics which keep people coming back to your profile

What is Instagram Stories?

Instagram stories let you post pictures and videos that vanish after 24 hours. Your content is neatly packaged together in a slide show format, so it is almost like creating your own mini-movie.

It is an excellent alternative to posting images and videos on your feed. Not only will your story keep your followers super engaged, but it can bring them back to your profile to like more of your content.

You will find Instagram stories across the top of your feed. The most recently posted stories will always appear on the far left. The oldest ones, or the ones you have viewed, will move further down to the right.

Instagram stories are important because it is a direct portal into your day to day life. The more your followers see you, the more trust you build with them. The more trust you develop, the more influence you have, and your influence is what companies will pay you for!

Instagram Stories: Do's and Don'ts

DO: Post daily.

Post an Instagram story several times a day. There is no hard and fast rule around what time to post. Some research suggests that peak times are between 11 am and 1 pm then again between 7 pm and 9 pm.

DON'T: Overdo it with animations and decorations.

There are tons of fun animations you can use in your story, so it is super easy to get carried away. Avoid this mistake!

DO: Post quality content

No matter what you post in your stories, bring an element of value each time.

DON'T: Write your text too small.

That is a mistake people make all the time, and it makes your followers disengaged. Make your text nice and big. Sometimes you may want to write something which is longer than a few lines. That is fine but be creative and spread it over a few story posts instead of cramming into one post.

DO: Be creative.

Instagram Stories are a canvas for creativity. Even if it means keeping up to date on other people's Instagram stories do it! As a story artist, you will need as much inspiration as possible.

DON'T: Be negative or abusive!

As an influencer, you will have your critics. There is not an influencer out there who has not had their fair share of haters. Do not use your influence to be negative or abusive towards these people. Companies looking to pay people to promote their products will avoid anyone who is obnoxious or offensive.

DO: Use Hashtags and Geotags.

That will blow up your reach and engagement. One smart way to add many hashtags to your stories is to use them in the same colour as your background and squeeze them small. Now push them in a corner where the audience is not likely to pay attention.

DO: Be transparent and build trust.

Posting content about your day to day life will build trust with your followers which is a high-end goal to have. The more confidence you build, the more of an influencer you are.

What to post to your Instagram story?

Your content strategy for your Instagram story goes hand in hand with the content strategy for your main feed. So, the nine categories of content that we discussed in the previous chapter will work for your stories as well. Let us do a quick recap of these:

1. The Selfie
2. What's Happening
3. Quotes
4. Humour
5. Short Videos
6. Trending Daily Hashtags
7. Behind the Scenes
8. Products in Use
9. The How-to Post

There is one more additional post category you must regularly use when posting a story. That category is known as the "call to action". Top influencers commonly use the story strategy right across Instagram and one you should use each time you add a new post to your feed.

So, what is it?

This strategy involves your sharing the content from your feed to your Instagram story but with the twist of creating a secret reveal. That prompts your followers (or anyone else who views your story) to visit your profile to see the content in full quickly.

That is a super powerful strategy that will drive hordes of people to your profile. However, do not overdo it. Try to use it only for your best images and videos.

Here is how it works!

Step 1: After you have uploaded content to your feed, click the "share button". It is the icon just above the caption, which looks like a little paper aeroplane. The share menu will appear, click "Add to Story".

Step 2: Here, you can decorate the post by covering the image.

Step 3: Add your strong "Call to Action". In this case, there are two - "Tap Here to Find Out", and the "Tap Here" gif, which is animated. When the user taps the screen, it will link them straight back to the original post, and all will be revealed.

This tactic stirs up real anticipation with your followers, and they will be eager to visit your profile to find out more. You can do this with selfies, how-to posts, quotes etc. You can do this with almost all content you post, and it is a super powerful way to keep your followers guessing!

Top 10 Tips to Quickly Create super-Engaging Stories

Tip #1: Use Coloured Backgrounds

Creating colour backgrounds is a smart little way to brighten up your story post. It is simple to do, check it out!

Step 1: Open your story and take a picture of anything. (it does not matter what)

Step 2: Hit the pen icon in the top right-hand corner, so the colour palette appears across the bottom of the screen.

Step 3: Choose the colour you like.

Step 4: Tap and hold the screen until the entire background changes colour.

Told you it was simple!

Tip #2: Carve Out Images

Carving out an image is a brilliant way to get your viewers to focus on just one part of your image. It is simple too!

Step 1: Open your story and choose an image you want to post.

Step 2: Now fill the screen with colour.

Step 3: The colour will now fill the screen, but your image will still be behind it.

Step 4: Choose the eraser function across the top of the screen and start to erase parts of the screen which will display some of the uploaded images.

And there you have it! You have carved out an image.

Tip #3: Drop shadow your text

A great way to make your story text stand out is to create a drop shadow. It is simple yet extremely unique. Here is how it works.

Step 1: Open your story and choose your background. It can be an image, video or colour background.

Step 2: Write your text choosing the colour you want and the size you want. Duplicate the text by using the copy and paste function. Resize each line of text, so they are the same size.

Step 3: Now layer the text on top of each other but slightly off centre. That gives you a cool shadow background which makes your text look 3D.

You can do these 3 or 4 times for extra effect.

Have a play around with different colour schemes and fonts when trying it out.

Tip #4: Type Letters Individually

This effect is incredible, and the best part is, not many accounts use it, so it will make your stories stand out from the rest. It will take you a little bit longer, but the effect is well worth it.

Step 1: Choose your image, video or background

Step 2: Type each letter of your caption individually

Step 3: Position the letters to make your caption

Again, it is all about experimenting, but you get the idea. When using this technique, you could try different fonts, add a drop shadow, write your words horizontally or vertically. Give it a go on your next story.

Tip #5: Mix Your Fonts Up

Another great way to captivate your story viewers is by mixing up your font selection. In the Instagram story mode, you are limited to only five fonts. These are Neon, Typewriter, Strong, Classic and Modern.

What to Post on Your Highlight Reel?

Your highlight reel will evolve as you evolve as an influencer. But the list below will help you kickstart your creativity for generating fantastic highlights.

Step 1: Add A Welcome Message

A great start is to add a simple welcome message for your profile visitors! People love this. Some research was conducted, which shows that a highlight welcome message can increase followers by 67%, that is amazing! Add a simple "hello", tell the visitor who you are, what your profile offers and do not forget to add a strong call to action in there and ask them to follow you.

Step 2: How-To

Whenever you post a "how-to" story, you are providing valuable information to your followers. You do not want to lose that information because it is pure gold to anyone who follows and admires you. Use these "how-to" stories to create permanent tutorials which will be right at the top of your profile for all to see.

Step 3: Blog Posts

A highlight reel is a great tool for creating a blog! You might find yourself on vacation for two weeks in Canada. Create a highlight reel dedicated to your vacation. Show off the beaches and local landmarks, show the world what an amazing place it is. Create a highlight reel dedicated to your cat or your workout regime or your morning routine. Whatever your niche is, create a highlight reel for it.

Step 4: AMA (Ask Me Anything)

Another amazing category for your highlight reel is the "AMA" which stands for "ask me anything". As the number of your followers will grow, so will the number of questions you receive. Use any question you get asked to create an "AMA" highlight reel. Your followers will love to find out more about you which in turn can boost your engagement and your influence!

Step 5: Create Your Episode

Thanks to the highlight reel, you can create hundreds of your niche episodes. Things like interviews, products, partners. You can create a reel about your family, your morning routine, your gym routine, your dog, your cat or even progress on the guitar lessons you are having.

Before You Start Creating Your Highlight Reel

Before you can upload a post to your highlight reel, you need to upload the post to your story. Instagram has a "Save To Archive" feature which we recommend you activate. That will save your story posts to the cloud, meaning you will never lose a single piece of content. To do this simply open your Instagram app and click "Settings". Then follow this path:

Setting > Privacy > Story > Save To Archive

Adding a highlight reel to your profile could not be easier.

On your profile, you should see a circle with a "+" symbol in the centre. Tapping this icon will take you to your story archive. Here you can choose a post to add to your highlight reel. Remember that the last post you select from your archive will be the first post in your highlight reel.

Adding A Highlight Name

All new highlights will need to have a name and icon associated with it. The name of your highlight should be no more than nine characters long. So, aim to keep the name of your highlight short and sweet.

Adding A Highlight Icon

When it comes to adding a highlight icon, you have two options - Add an image from your camera or photo library as an icon. Make your icon.

We recommend the second option. Creating your highlight cover will keep the look and feel of your Instagram profile page consistent with your overall Instagram aesthetic.

Try to make sure that your icon represents the highlight reel as much as possible. If your highlight is about music, then use a musical note. If the reel is about travel, use an aeroplane, etc.

Canva is a great tool to create your custom made highlight covers. You can also find some free highlight covers using the link below:

Instagram Live

Instagram Live is a fantastic feature which allows you to live stream directly from your device your followers. It is just liked a live TV channel! It is a fantastic way to bolster trust with your followers, interact with them live and find out more about what they want to see from you.

As soon as you go live, your followers will receive a notification inviting them to watch you. If you want to stand out above the rest of the influencers in your niche, and become one of the top earners, then this tool is an absolute must for you.

How to start an Instagram Live broadcast

Starting an Instagram Live broadcast is easy. Let us walk through how to broadcast live and review some of the other features you can use when broadcasting to your followers.

Step 1: Once your Instagram app is open, click the camera icon in the top left corner. That will take you to your Instagram story page.

Step 2: You should now see a menu across the bottom of the screen — slide over to the "Live" option. Then hit "Go Live".

Instagram will check your connection before the broadcast begins. Congratulations! You are now live.

Step 3: To end your broadcast, you just need to hit "End" in the top right corner.

Instagram Live has some cool features once your broadcast begins, and you can find these across the bottom of your screen.

Comments

The comments field allows you to type comments live to your viewers. Your broadcast will be a bit like a chat room but with your live video playing in the background. Your viewers can ask your questions which will be viewed here. That option allows you to direct message to people who follow you or watch your live broadcast.

Split broadcast function

That is awesome for engagement! This option allows you to share a broadcast with a friend, followers or associates. It is excellent if you are in partnership with people in your niche.

Filters

This option lets you add screen filters which are great for entertainment.

Add Image option

This option lets you add an image to your broadcast. That will come in handy when promoting products or services.

What should you broadcast?

There are different types of broadcasts you can create to keep your followers engaged. It is a good idea to plan your broadcasts ahead of time, so you do not look unorganised. With that said, do not worry about creating the perfect broadcast. Just get out there and engage with your followers.

Use some of the following formats to get yourself started on Instagram Live:

The How-to Broadcast

That is a great way to inform your followers of something in your niche. The "how-to" broadcast brings value to your followers, and the more value you bring, the more trust you build. If people are getting something out of you, then they are more likely to continue watching.

AMA (Ask Me Anything)

AMA sessions are great for engagement and something you could do as a standalone broadcast. You could also run an AMA during or directly after a how-to broadcast.

Behind the scenes

Are you out shopping, eating or even relaxing at a friend's house? Then this would be a perfect time to broadcast a "behind the scenes" post. Show the world what you are doing and let them in on your day to day life.

Live Show or Live Events

Are You at a concert or event? Then you have another great opportunity to broadcast live. A live event is not just about attending concerts. A live show could be something as simple as a box opening broadcast. If your niche is fashion, then broadcast a box opening of those new shoes you just bought.

Interviews

Find people in your niche and interview them; this makes for a great broadcast. You can set a one on one interview or use the split broadcast function. The beauty of the split-screen broadcast is that you will get exposure to your interviewee's followers.

As you become a natural broadcaster, you may want to create more spur of the moment type broadcast. That is when you do not plan any particular broadcast, and you just put yourself out there and see what happens. Again, this is great for your followers and your engagement.

Monetising Your Instagram Influencer Profile

We will now look at the top 3 ways influencers earn on Instagram. These are:

1. Affiliate Schemes
2. Post for Product Partnerships
3. Paid Collaboration Partnerships

Affiliate Schemes

An affiliate scheme is a programme most reputable companies offer. You can usually join a company's affiliate scheme quite easily. Most companies have a link to their affiliate scheme at the bottom of their website. If they do not, then it will be a case of contacting them to request information on how to join.

Once you join, you will receive a unique link to their website, which you will use to promote. The link they give will be unique to you, so whenever a follower uses that link to visit the company website. The company will know that the customer came from your promotional work and they will pay you a commission should the follower make a purchase.

Commission amounts vary depending on the company you chose to promote. Some pay only 1% of commission others pay 50%. Most of the time, these commission amounts are set and non-negotiable. So, you need to check what the company is offering. Otherwise, it will not be worth your time and effort.

Before you decide to go for affiliate schemes, you need to understand that promoting affiliates are not generally profitable unless you have a lot of followers and a high engagement rate. That is because, when it comes to commission, most affiliate schemes pay on the lower end of the scale. So, make sure you check out what the company is offering before deciding whether to promote an affiliate.

Post for Product Partnerships

Post for product partnerships are precisely that; you generate a post for a company in exchange for the product they are selling. No money is exchanged; instead, you get to keep the product as payment and Hey get their product exposed to your followers. Simple as that!

Post for product offers can be great and will most likely be the first offer types you receive as an Instagram influencer. Lots of smaller businesses use this route as an excellent way to get their products out there. The best thing is, they are ready to make deals with influencers right now.

Depending on how much the product is valued at will determine what effort you should put into promoting it. We will discuss more pricing and contracts later in the book. However, understand that if a product is valued at $10, then you are not going to create 30 posts over a month for it. Your account, your following and your influence are worth so much more than that.

Post for the product is a great way to start as an influencer. It will give you experience in building business relationships, negotiating post requirements and promoting products. However, do not get overwhelmed when the offers start to roll in. You need to be meticulous in who you choose to work with. When you receive an offer, do your research on the company and ask yourself the following questions:

- Does the product fit my niche and what I am representing?
- Is this a product I would genuinely need and use?
- Is this product something my followers would be interested in?
- Does the company have any bad press or negative reviews from paying customers?
- Does the company have ethical values which align with mine?

Instead of losing time in wait for companies to connect with you for product offers, be proactive and look for companies which offer products you like or even buy from. Reach out and ask them to use you as part of their marketing campaign.

There is more about how to approach companies later. But understand that this is hugely effective because companies know the power of influence and are desperate for right trustworthy influencers like you.

Paid Collaboration Partnerships

Paid collaboration partnership is another way of saying "paid ad". You promote a product or service to your followers in exchange for money. That is the reason you want to be as an influencer!

If post for product suits the smaller company, then you will find the medium to large companies go down the route of paid collaboration. The reason for this is that the medium to large companies now have specific departments dedicated to social media. Within those departments comes a budget which is used to pay for promotion. Because influencer marketing is becoming an extremely effective way of selling products, a large portion of this budget goes on finding and paying high-quality influencers to promote products and services.

You need to use all the skills from this playbook to improve your chances of tapping into that budget. Just like with post for a product, companies will reach out to you, and when they do, you will need to research the company and ask yourself the same questions:

- Does the product fit my niche and what I am representing?
- Is this a product I would genuinely need and use?
- Is this product something my followers would be interested in?
- Does the company have any bad press or negative reviews from paying customers?
- Does the company have ethical values which align with mine?

Finding Companies to Partner With

As an influencer with a super highly engaged following, you will receive partnership offerings from all kinds of companies. However, it is not a recommended strategy to sit back and "wait for the offers to roll in". Finding good companies to partner with is a real hustle. But fear not, there are two great ways to find companies you want to partner with. Here they are:

1. Find influencers in your niche and see what products they are promoting.

The first reason you should do this is that the products being promoted are already in your niche. You should only aim to promote products in your niche because it aligns with your followers' needs. The second reason you should do this is that the company is already taking full advantage of the influencer marketing industry. They will have a budget ready to partner with highly engaging influencers like you!

2. Search Instagram for products that you use or products that you would use.

Are you a fashion influencer? Then look for clothing companies that sell products you love the look of. Are you a fitness influencer? Then look for sportswear, nutrition and any other companies relating to fitness. The beauty of this is that these companies are using Instagram to promote and create engagement about their brand. They completely understand the power that influencers like you have to engage people and develop sales for them.

Why you Should Approach Companies for Partnership Deals

As your follower base grows and your influence increases, you will get contacted about new potential partnership deals. However, this is what you should do – be as proactive as possible and reach out to companies about a partnership. Do not sit back and rely on them contacting you. Here is why:

1. The influencer industry is growing, so you want to let companies know who you are and what you are available for partnership deals.

2. Reaching out to companies about partnership deals will get you ahead of your competitors. (i.e. other Instagram influencers in your niche)

3. The influencer industry is growing so medium to large companies do not need to seek out new influencers. That is because influencers are contacting them daily.

4. Even if a company does not want to offer you a partnership deal now, it does not mean they will not participate in the future. They will keep your details which could turn into big $$$ later on down the line.

Influencer marketing is still at a nascent stage, and some companies have not woken up to its true potential just yet. With that in mind, don't lose your confidence or focus when you receive a message back saying thanks but no thanks." You will get rejected by companies, and that is absolutely natural. That is a numbers game so the more companies you contact, the more chances you have of landing that first paid collaboration deal.

How to Approach Companies for Partnership Deals?

The best way to approach a company about a potential partnership deal is through, you guessed it, Instagram. There are three main reasons for this:

Reason #1

The person who makes the decisions around who to partner with will usually be in charge of the social media account. So mostly, you will be direct messaging the person who can say yes or no to a potential partnership deal.

Reason #2

By messaging via Instagram, the company can instantly view your account and all of your quality content. They will be able to see who you are, what you stand for, and why you will be a great fit to promote their products or services.

Reason #3

The company is active on Instagram, which proves they understand the power of Instagram influence.

Before you approach any company about potential partnership deals, you will need to get extremely familiar with your audience stats. That can be found in your "insights" page under the "audience" tab. That and your engagement rate are the two main pieces of information which companies will want before considering you for a partnership deal.

When you send a message, keep it friendly and professional. Explain who you are, what your niche is, and why you like their products. Then give them all the information from your audience" page including age, range, locations and gender split. Then go on to explain what your engagement rate is over your last ten posts.

You want to position your message in a way that excites the company. So, what excites companies you ask? Money!

Money excites companies so stick a dollar next to your engagement rate. For example, if your engagement rate is 3% which equals likes for 450 followers. Then explain that one post from your account could equal 450 sales! Do not be afraid to sell yourself.

What to Charge and Creating Your Price List

You can quite quickly charge $75 - $100 per image for every 10,000 followers you have. That based on an engagement rate of around 3%. That does not add in the fact that you can offer amazing videos, stories, highlights and Instagram Live posts either. We are talking a base rate of $75 - $100 per image post for every 10,000 followers with 3% engagement. Keep that figure firmly in your mind.

Each method of posting can be charged at a different rate. That is because each process will take longer for you to create and have different levels of engagement and effectiveness.

When to Charge Companies

When you start charging real money is down to you. You can start asking for monetary compensation immediately. You can also go down the route of post for the product until your confident enough to set a dollar price for your services.

Just remember that you are offering more than only exposure to potential buyers. You are offering brand awareness to a follower base who trust you as an influencer. That's 1000x more powerful than any TV or radio advertisement.

Going down the post for product route is a wise move to start with as it gets you used to negotiate deals with limited commitment. Plus, you can begin contacting smaller companies about a post for product partnerships with as little of 3,000 followers.

When you first create a contract with a company. You will need to be extremely specific about the terms of that contract. It is always good to agree the following before creating any posts for a company.

1. What content or content package does the company want to purchase?
2. Have they agreed on the price?
3. How will payment be made? Confirm when content will be posted
4. Does the company have any requirements within the content? For example, how do they want the product displayed in the content, etc.?
5. How long will the campaign last?
6. Does the company want to be tagged into the post? If so, how?
7. Does the company want exclusivity?

What Is Exclusivity?

Some companies request exclusivity when entering into a paid collaboration. What this means is that the company wants you to promote their products and no one else's products for an agreed period. For example, say a company wants to pay you $1500 to create eight posts (2 per week) over a month. They may request that you do not promote any other products or services for other companies during that month.

Basically, they want you all to themselves!

Further to this, exclusivity means they may want full rights to the content you create. When you agree to this, you allow the company to use that content in any way they chose. They could repost it on their social media pages, add it to their website or use it in YouTube ads etc.

Exclusivity is not necessarily a bad thing, and it could lead to some fantastic business relationships. However, make sure you understand what the company's definition of exclusivity Is. And do not forget to confirm how long they want their exclusivity period to last.

f you are in a paid partnership, then it is a legal requirement to disclose the fact that you are being paid to promote products or services. Some countries have strict advertising standards, whereas others do not. You will need to contact your countries advertising standards agency for advice.

f you do not have time for that, then there are two straightforward ways to make sure you are compliant with advertising legislation.

1. Hashtags

   You can readily disclose your partnership by merely using hashtags #sponsored #spon #paid #ad #partnership. These are all internationally recognised hashtags which admit full disclosure so use them all when either posting for a product or for a paid partnership

2. Tagging

   Another effortless way to ensure that you satisfy all disclosure laws is by simply tagging in the company you are partnered with.

Make sure you are open, honest and transparent whenever you are promoting a paid partnership. The last thing you want is contact with your government advertising standards agency!

There have been cases where influencers have gotten themselves banned from influencing on Instagram. So, do not get caught out. Do not be put off by disclosure either, just use the above two techniques to ensure you are fully disclosing your intentions to promote.

Introduction to YouTube

With the advent of YouTube in 2005, it became one of the most significant game-changers of the Internet. It was beneficial to video producers, entertainment industrialists, and casting agents. They could now easily find sources of talent. If videos became a mega-hit, the producers and agents contacted the video uploader to sign record deals and contracts.

Since YouTube's inception, several "YouTube celebrities" have ended up becoming a worldwide phenomenon due to their homegrown talent. Many Hollywood companies and record labels have also been on the constant lookout and have partnered with YouTube for this very purpose. Celebrities have given several comedians, bloggers, and singers recognition, one notable example being Justin Bieber through Usher. Several celebrities also created channels to increase their fame.

Celebrities who were conventionally popular through traditional media also received invitations from the team at YouTube to upload videos, increasing the amount of traffic to the site and growing their target audience and followers to a far greater extent than what they obtained through their TV shows and movies.

In the year 2006, YouTube also partnered with NBC and promoted TV shows aired by NBC. Following this came the purchase of YouTube by Google, for $1.65 billion. That served as an excellent platform to market products, and advertising companies flocked the scene. Thus, marketing professionals of big companies fled from the television screen to the Internet.

Soon YouTube became customer-driven and business-driven. Independent artists, singers, and comedians were able to milk the crowd with the little-to-no cost. Four big record labels came into play though they were all very apprehensive given the large amount of copyrighted content that was on the site. YouTube provided a platform to these big record label companies by creating a partnership with them. The lucrative offer was that the site served as a base to make more money for these record labels. In

2009, YouTube partnered with Vivendi and formed Vevo. Vevo was a music service video channel.

YouTube also provided a platform for several channels to increase their profits by investing $875,000 in NextUp, which was a training and tips program for prospective users of YouTube. The company also used celebrities and icons to promote the channel, hoping to get the best of both worlds.

YouTube also was a free platform to test and promote music labels. Videos were categorised as mega, mainstream, and mid-sized, which got rave reviews from target audiences. With this, recording artists could test songs before releasing them for free. That increased the number of hits. YouTube also made its policies very strict as its popularity grew. In 2014, YouTube started to block videos from labels that flouted rules and were not a part of the paid subscription, and they lead to bad reviews and loss of profits.

Today, YouTube is the creator's paradise. Let us take you there.

Beginning with YouTube

Creating a YouTube channel is the easiest of all the tasks you must do in reaching your final goal. So, let us get right to it. Following is a 3-step process to achieving this feat:

Step 1: Create a google account

Step 2: Decide a name for your channel

Step 3: Customize your channel

Step 1: Creating a Google Account

This step is relevant only to those who are yet to own a Google account. If you already have an account, you can skip this step (that is, creating a Google account).

You must note here that using YouTube is exclusive to Google users only, so you must have a Google account. Yahoo or other accounts are not accepted on YouTube. In case, you do not have an account yet, open your web browser and visit https://www.mail.google.com and click on "Create account".

Fill all the required details and choose a secure password. When you are done with all those, accept the Google Terms and Conditions and click "Finish". Once your account is made, log in on your browser and start enjoying all of Google's products and services.

To access YouTube, visit https://www.youtube.com. YouTube uses your Google username as your YouTube username by default. But before you sign in on YouTube for the first time, you will be required to supply your first and last names. These names will be used as you Identification on YouTube. So, it depends on you if you wish to use your real name or something else.

Step 2: Deciding on a Name for Your Channel

The success of your channel is contingent on the choice of name for it. It could be confusing at times to decide on what name you would use to identify your channel. There is no principle or sets of instructions that place restrictions on what you can and cannot use as your channel's name. However, a good name could be a source of the traffic to your channel (although not all the time), as well as a good description of your channel and what it represents. So, think about it thoroughly.

There are two methods adopted by popular YouTubers for naming their channels – using their real names and using their brand names.

You must be creative about this. Here are a few tips you could adopt in coming up with an interesting brand name for your channel:

Alliteration

t is an effortless way to come up with a brand name which sometimes also gives interesting and memorable brand names. Examples of such brand names are PayPal, Coca-Cola, Dunkin' Donuts, Best Buy and Charisma on Command.

Rhymes

Many famous brand names were coined using rhymes. Rhymes are quite like alliterations. However, they differ in that alliteration is characterised by similar consonant sounds while rhymes may use the consonant sounds, or the vowel sounds or both at the same time. An example of a popular channel name coined by rhyming is PewDiePie.

Single-word

You could use a single word you feel describes or represents what your brand stands for as a channel name. It could be descriptive or non-descriptive or just a word you like, anything. Remember you are at liberty to choose whatever you prefer as your channel name.

Step 3: Customizing your channel

Your channel's appearance gives off its first impression and can be a basis to keep or lose viewers. People prefer to see something that appeals to their taste, and so you must consider what would be more attractive to your viewers. The options available for you to customise your channel are:

- The Icon
- The Art
- The Description

The Icon

Your channel icon is the first crucial customisable option available to you. It is what people see beside your channel name even before they open your channel. The photo can be a photo of yourself or a logo. You could also have your photograph converted to paper art by professional designers; it is a quite popular move by YouTubers. It looks good even on people that are not ridiculously photogenic.

The Art

This refers to your banner which sits like a horizontal bar at the top of your channel page. You could have a professional designer design one for you on freelance networks for as low as $5. You can also use royalty-free stock photos from anywhere on the internet.

The Description

The description offers a summary of what your channel stands for. Although few actual subscribers care enough to read channel description, you would not want to lose subscribers because you did not do well in this area.

Here you can add links to your other relevant social media profiles, websites, business email, a featured channels section, a Frequently Asked Questions (FAQ) section and a channel trailer.

A channel trailer gives people an idea of what to expect and what they will experience on your channel. It is a visual presentation of your past channel activities. You can feature here your most popular content to deliver an impression.

Time to Upload Videos

Uploading videos is easy. After logging in, all you need do is click the upload button at the top-right corner of your YouTube page. Now, you can drag your video and drop her or click that large upload button to browse for videos on your device. You could use the import option - this allows you to upload videos you have saved to the cloud, for example, Google Photos.

The scheduling feature allows you to upload your videos in advance and put them on auto-publish at a specified time in future.

Important points to note

1. People can view only those videos which you make public. If you set them on private mode, only you will be able to see them or those with whom you have shared a direct link to that video.

2. When scheduling videos, you set the time where the videos go from either private or unlisted to public and automatically the videos status changes at the scheduled time and date.

3. The maximum size of the video to be uploaded on an up-to-date browser is 128GB. If your browser is not updated, then you might be able to upload a maximum of 20GB.

4. YouTube accounts that are yet to be verified cannot upload videos longer than 15 minutes. The limit gets removed after you verify your account.

To avoid getting an error message like "invalid file format", upload videos in mp4 format. There are many video converters online that you could use to convert your video from whatever format to the acceptable format.

How to Make Good Content on YouTube

The typical YouTube audience is 13-35 years old, and they are looking for engaging content with a lot of value to offer. So, your content should be captivating and flashy. However, if you are aiming for an older demographic, these people may watch videos up to several hours in length, if they are engaging.

The King of content length, though is the ten-minute video. A ten-minute video is not too short to be sparse and is not too long to be boring. If you pack your video with exciting and engaging content, aim for a video length between five to fifteen minutes but pick whatever is best for your content. If you are making ultra-short comedy videos, these might be less than three minutes in length and if you are uploading your lectures, these might be hours long!

Here are the most popular types of content on YouTube:

Comedy videos

They are some of the most shared videos on the internet as they keep the audience pleasantly occupied. These are often fast-paced and with a high energy level. If you wish to create comedy videos, there are two ways to go about it:

The first method is to be the most extroverted and outgoing version of yourself. Its scientifically proven people are going to listen to things that are loud and things that change quickly, and these are principles you need to embed into your videos. A monotone monologue just is not going to cut it!

It is a proven fact these types of channels have a higher number of subscribers than most network's comedy television shows, which is crazy to think about.

Though the sense of humour is personal, there are a lot of comedy videos online, and you can be sure you will find somebody who matches your style. Remember, do not be afraid to be inspired by the style of another YouTuber, but add your own personality and flair to your videos.

Unboxing videos

Though this might come as a surprise, it turns out that there are lots of people interested in watching someone else remove a new product from its packing. Think about when you buy something new that you have wanted for a prolonged period, the excitement that you have when you finally open it, that great feeling of self-esteem and joy.

If you can transfer that through a screen to your followers, you are already on your way to thousands of subscribers.

Finding Stuff to Unbox

The truth is, people, do like to see expensive and upcoming items reviewed. An effective way to find these items is to type in your product name into YouTube and see if there is a market for it. In addition, if you ever see a video and think "I can do better than that" then you can. That is what finding a niche is all about.

Your product does not have to be expensive. In fact, it is counterproductive to start reviewing costly products in the beginning. But your passion is essential.

Product reviews

You can also do product review videos, and this opens an opportunity for you to make a lot of money in the future by doing sponsored review videos, especially if you have a large subscriber base.

Most people want to know other people's opinions about the products they want to buy before they buy them. Pick something you know a lot about. People will listen to you if you know a lot about something and can bring that confidence and passion across.

If your video is positive, then they will want to make a purchase. A smart way to leverage this fact to make money is by using Amazon Affiliates. That is an incredible way to bolster your income from YouTube.

Since lots of people go on YouTube in search of reviews for the products they want to buy, try making reviews on a product that people do not have videos on. A beyond excellent way to check what people are looking for is to type the product in on Google AdSense and check how many searches it has. If a product has many searches on AdSense but no videos on YouTube, then you have struck gold.

Gaming Videos

If one niche dominates YouTube, it is undoubtedly this. PewDiePie, the biggest YouTuber, started with this niche! That can be like an unboxing video; in that, you are showing people a game that they have never played before.

What is unique about this, though is that you inject your personality into the video to enhance the game. People want to see your unique reactions to whatever is going on. Pick a game, or a genre of games and stick to them.

Remember, the essential thing in this equation is you and your reactions. A secret technique to increase your viewers and subscribers, especially if you are a PC gamer, is to find an indie game on Steam that is upcoming and message the developer by email asking for a copy before the game is released.

Even if you do not have a lot of subscribers, if your videos are quality, then most reasonable game developers will say yes. If they say no, however, you can wait until the game is released and review it later. If the dev features your video and the game is successful, this can increase your subscribers and grow your channel like crazy.

Live Streaming

Live Streaming is also great for creating engagement between you and your viewers. That is excellent for getting donations and live feedback on how you are doing. You do not have to be good at whichever video game you are playing; however, this is where your personality must shine through.

Since this type of streaming typically involves a webcam or camera or some sort, make sure you are comfortable and confident in front of a camera. Remember, practice makes perfect.

Vlogs

The classic YouTube videos. The concept is simple. You shoot a video talking to the camera about any random topic. People want a window into your life. They want to know what you are like, all your nuances. The more you can open while keeping the video engaging, the better.

Pro tips for vlogs

1. White rooms reflect light much better than dark rooms, so try and film in a light environment

2. Good lighting is necessary. You can buy a ring light inexpensively from Amazon

3. Be positive. In life, it takes effort to be a good person and say positive things on camera, and people want to be uplifted and forget about the stressful day they have had in general.

4. Finding a niche is especially important. There are many channels with excellent video quality, but they do not have many subscribers simply because their niche is just too competitive, and they are unaware of the tips in this book.

Educational / How-to

In 2019, the amount of traffic to these kinds of videos increased by 70%, that means the views these videos got nearly doubled. Imagine how much this will increase during 2020.

If you are good at something or know how to do it, you can give tutorials on YouTube. It is simple; in fact, you do not even have to be good at something. Look at How to Basic as an example of this fact. Whether it is Mathematics tutorials (which is a hugely growing niche on YouTube) or underwater basket weaving, there are countless things that people need help on.

Other types of content include haul videos, memes, Top 10 compilations and the infamous prank videos. Of course, there are an infinite number of video types that exist, and if you do not see your kind here, do not dismay.

One of the biggest keys in being able to grow with any online platform is learning how the algorithms work so you can begin leveraging the algorithm

The YouTube algorithm is unlike other algorithms, which tends to favour things that have been seen or liked more than it favours viewing time. That is because YouTube is amongst the only video viewing platforms that offer full-service video watching and is entirely dedicated to video-based content. So, along with building a fantastic marketing strategy and using high-quality content, you also need to know how to work the algorithm to generate the success that you desire in the online space.

The Importance of Frequency

On YouTube, one of the most important things that you can do for your growth is to publish the latest content for your viewers consistently. Many people forget that YouTube is a social media website, which means it favours accounts that are engaging in regular sharing back and forth. The more frequently you upload to your channel and have friends and viewers engaging with your videos, the more YouTube is going to favour your content and drive you up in the rankings when it comes to people searching for your content.

You might get a lot of hits early on, but if you do not maintain your frequency, the content that you share will stop getting views. You need to keep your momentum and continue growing it if you are going to generate continued success with YouTube, which means that you need to ensure that you are consistently uploading videos.

Another massive benefit of frequently uploading new content is that you are driving new traffic to your channel consistently. That means that not only will your new videos get visibility, but you will also increase the visibility of older ones. As people land on your videos, they will hopefully take the next step and visit your channel to see what other videos you offer. Through that process, if you have plenty of high-quality videos uploaded that are relevant to your niche, these individuals will click-through to your older videos and watch them as well. The more they do this, the higher your older videos will rank and the better your overall channel will rank as well, which means that your growth rate will increase exponentially

Creating a consistent frequency is best done if you create a posting schedule and then adhere to that schedule as you grow your channel. If you look at any mature channel that presently exists on YouTube, chances are, their posting schedule is listed directly on their intro clip, or they say it when they introduce themselves at the beginning of each video.

These schedules ensure that your audience knows how often to check back for recent videos and gives them an idea to how frequently you are uploading updated content. It also keeps you on a consistent schedule so that you know exactly how often you need to be uploading without falling behind or creating an inconsistency that leaves your audience constantly questioning as to when they will see you next. You should seek to be uploading at least once per week, but two or three times is preferable if you want to grow your channel quickly as this will give your viewers plenty to watch when they find you online.

What YouTube Cares About

While frequency is important in terms of relevance and visibility, there is one other thing that YouTube cares about when it comes to a ranking - number of watch-time minutes. Watch-time minutes refer to the length of video that those who are landing on your video are watching. In other words, if people are watching your videos all the way through, or at least are watching them longer than any other videos in your similar search terms, then you are going to get listed higher in the feed.

So, as a YouTube content creator, your primary objectives, aside from creating consistent and high-quality content, are creating content that encourages people to stick around and watch your videos all the way through.

The reason YouTube favours watch times is that it means that your content is exciting and that people are enjoying watching it. When your watch time is low, YouTube assumes that you are offering low-quality or uninteresting content that will bore their members and leave them, unwilling to return to watch more creators in the future.

Calculation of average viewing time

Average watch time = Total watched minutes / Total viewers

For example, you have 100 watch time minutes, and you have had 25 unique viewers. So, the average watch time for your video would be 4 minutes.

YouTube will then rank you lower than anyone who has experienced at 4:01 watch time or higher, and higher than anyone who has experienced a 3:59 watch time or lower.

Your goal is to improve your watch time to get it as close to 100% so that YouTube starts favouring your videos and ranks them above anyone else's.

Encouraging Higher Watch Times

You can increase your overall watch time by considering the importance of creating relevant and high-quality content. There are additional things that you can do to improve your total watch time, as well.

1. Offer an incentive to stay till the end of the video, such as a summary to a story that you have started, or a giveaway offer that they can gain by watching your video all the way through. When you offer an incentive like this, make sure that you mention it early on an allude to it throughout the video in order for people stay interested in what it is and continue to watch so they can learn more about the incentive or hear it all the way through.

2. Fill your videos with valuable information that is relevant to your viewers and share it interestingly. Do not create an annoying video that struggles to get to the point or that has been watered down.

3. Keep your videos reasonable in length for people not to grow bored or disinterested purely based on the duration of the video. The length of your audience's attention span will ultimately depend on what you are talking about, so consider searching your niche market and getting a feel for approximately

how long the videos are. Try and stay fairly like the median length, so you are not exceeding it by too much and losing the interest of people along the way.

4. Another way to increase your viewership is by structuring your playlists. As you begin to develop more videos, you can group your videos in playlists for your audience to watch. If you arrange these videos into playlists linearly or in a sensical way, your viewers can watch your videos and continue watching them through.

5. You have seen this before, but a fantastic way to encourage further views and to retain an interest in your videos and your channel is to make use of "cards." For example, say you just showed your audience how to fix a tire, and now you want to show them how they can pack a proper safety kit for emergencies in their trunk. These two would be highly relevant to each other, so using cards to reference the opposite video when the current video ends would be a great way to encourage your viewers to move back and forth between both videos. That works almost like a - funnel on YouTube where you drive "hot leads" through a series of your videos and, based on their current interests and their retained viewership, you can almost guarantee that they will watch more of your videos all the way, too.

Lastly, make sure that your videos are being titled and described adequately so that people know what to expect when they watch your video, and they get precisely that.

Optimising Your SEO

Every single search engine that exists today, including YouTube, has an optimisation strategy that you can use to increase your ability to get found in the search rankings. It is called Search Engine Optimisation or SEO. That SEO strategy is different for every platform since the algorithms used to generate rankings will vary depending on what each algorithm is looking for.

YouTube favours high-quality content that is relevant, interesting, retains viewers, and gets consistent engagement from those who are actively watching it. You can increase the favourability of your videos in four steps:

Step 1: Creating an SEO plan

Step 2: Putting SEO into action

Step 3: Monitoring the performance through analytics

Step 4: Keeping up with the trends

Step 1: Creating an SEO Plan

Begin with keyword research

First, do some keyword research to get an idea of what people in your niche are looking for.

Start by writing down a list of potential keywords that are relevant to your video that you think will best describe what your audience can gain from watching it. The best way to populate this list is to go to the search bar and type in one or two words and then look at what comes up in the recommended search list. That list will be based on the most commonly searched topics on YouTube. So, choosing potential keywords from this list will make sure that you are likely to get seen by others.

Once you have generated your potential keyword list, you can go to any keyword research platform, such as Google Keywords, and started typing in those keywords in the search bar to see how they are ranking. Ones that are being searched frequently, such as tens or hundreds of thousands of times per month, can be considered as being popular enough to warrant actual results from. Ones that are not being searched often, such as the ones that are only being searched for a couple of hundred times or less, should be ignored as they are unlikely to generate your desired results. Furthermore, avoid those with search rankings over 500,000 views per month as these may get you washed out by your competitors who may already have a better viewership than you do.

Maintain high watch time

The next part of SEO is keeping all your videos high in retention as possible to avoid having YouTube believing that your audience is not interested in watching your videos. If you are getting started, ask your closest friends and family to watch your full video to get it a high viewership ranking right off the bat.

Enhance keyword relevance

Another thing that matters on YouTube, which people often forget is that you need to say your keywords aloud while you are filming the video that you are creating. YouTube will recognise that, and this looks positive in terms of your relevance.

Promote your videos

Share your video to every different platform that you are actively on and then encourage your followers to re-share the video if they feel that it is relevant or interesting. Not only does that get you more views, but it also helps YouTube recognise that your video as popular and interesting. The more inbound likes there are out on the net directing people to your videos, the higher your ranking is going to become because it is seen as exciting and relevant.

The higher these analytics grow, the more your channel will grow, so it is well worth your time to invest in these details and nurture your growth through SEO.

Step 2: Putting SEO into action

SEO is a complicated skill that is difficult to explain. There could easily be an entirely separate book on the subject. But the fact that it is not a natural skill to master is why those who understand it can gain success on YouTube.

Here are a few pointers to tweak your SEO:

1. The titles for the videos you post on your channel should include keywords that people will search. It is not a smart idea to make titles that abandon all creative integrity just for the sake of SEO. But whenever you are creating titles for videos, it should be kept in mind.

2. Making your titles exciting is an integral part of SEO. When people search for the keywords included in your title, they should want to click on your video because it is something they want to see.

3. Tag your videos properly. Tags are keywords you attach to your video so that YouTube knows what exactly is in your video and what categories it falls under. Let us say you have a YouTube channel all about birds and you want other people who love birds to find your videos. The smartest way to get this done is by adding tags to your videos that include keywords that bird lovers would be searching for on YouTube.

Step 3: Monitoring Your Analytics

Once you have begun posting and optimising content to be found by people on the internet, you will need to invest time analysing the performance of your content.

YouTube Analytics is a tool which is available, free of charge to anyone who has created content on YouTube. To access YouTube Analytics, you need to navigate to the Video Manager from within your channel. You will now see Analytics listed in the left-hand panel.

Your YouTube analytics tells you absolutely everything about your videos and your channel overall, allowing you to get a better insight as to what is working and what is not. Through your analytics, you can see what you need to do to improve your viewership and get better rankings, overall.

The first thing you want to monitor when you go to your YouTube analytics is your overall retained viewership ratings because this is what YouTube cares about the most. If this number is high, chances are the rest of your analytics are going to be higher as well.

Wouldn't it be lovely to know how many people watched your video in its entirety, or what the average duration of each view was? This information does not seem that interesting, but on closer inspection, it is enormously influential.

If one of your videos is only being viewed for the first 50%, what does this tell you? Are you losing the interest of your viewer or did you say something at 50% which has made the viewer turn off in disgust? Now you have these stats to hand; you can make informed decisions about how you choose to broadcast in future. Sure, it is nice knowing you have had 200 viewers on your video, but it is not so lovely knowing that half of them turned off in the middle of your video.

The beauty of YouTube Analytics is that you have this information at your fingertips and can act before it is too late. You can address such issues and ensure that your next broadcast does not make the same perceived errors like the one you are currently analysing.

YouTube Analytics also gives you a gender breakdown of your viewers. Now, this might not make any difference to you depending on what your broadcasts are about, but if your broadcasting style is on the assumption that the core of your audience is of a particular gender, you now have the raw data to back this up. You can now focus your presentation style to the gender of your audience which will allow you to attract more viewers from that gender or retain the viewers you currently have because you are now delivering content which you are more confident is relevant to them.

If you are broadcasting something of high complexity, which contains many small parts, users viewing on a mobile phone may not be getting the best experience of your broadcast due to the size of their screen. While this is beyond your control, it is worth knowing what kind of device your broadcasts are being viewed on.

When you read your analytics, make sure that you not only pay attention to your overall channel growth but to your video performance as well. The production of each video will tell you whether your strategies are working in each video, especially as your channel continues growing. As your channel grows and these numbers have a more extended history, you can start recognising the trends on your channel. That will give you a unique idea as to what your viewers like and what they do not like on your channel.

These trends will show you everything from what titles draw the most attention to what styles of videos keep your viewers watching the longest, and even what content gets the most views in general. You want to start producing more of the material that meets these three criteria:

- receives the highest views,
- with the highest retention ratings, and the best engagement ratings.

So, the videos that have many people clicking through to watch it, that have people watching it all the way through, and that have people liking or commenting on or subscribing to your channel are the videos that you want to favour.

You should not exclusively pay attention to your high-performing videos, either, as this will leave money on the table. When you have a video that underperforms or that does not meet the expectations that you had for it, take some time to research it and look through its analytics to see what may have gone wrong. Pay attention to how you may have unintentionally sabotaged the video or prevented it from growing and see if you can improve on these things or avoid them altogether in the future.

Step 4: Keeping up with the Trends

If your YouTube channel aims to discuss topical items, you are going to need to keep up to date with breaking news and viral themes. As we have already discussed, delivering content that the viewer wants is paramount to the success of your YouTube channel. So, you are going to need a way of finding out what fellow YouTubers are watching and talking about so that you can strike while the topic is still hot.

YouTube Trends is another free tool that is available publicly that allows you to see what the most popular videos currently are in terms of both views and shares. That data, as with the YouTube Analytics tool, can be dissected further so that you can see on a country by country basis what is popular. You can also break down the trend data by age or by gender, so if you have a target audience in mind, and you now have the information of what this demographic is demanding from YouTube.

While YouTube Trends give you vital information on what viewers are enjoying; you should not automatically jump away from the focus of your channel. Visiting Trends, just before you are about to record your next broadcast, is always a good tactic. If you find something is trending that you can work into your video, then there is an increased chance that your video could be shared, thus giving it more exposure.

Remember, today's trend is yesterday's news so if you plan to use trend topics in your broadcast. You need to act immediately.

Most of your time will go into producing your videos. There are two sets of tools that you will need to create your channel. First, you will need the tools that you will use make and edit your videos before you upload them to YouTube. Second, you will need a constant source of content. In the case of YouTube, content refers to events that you film and edit. Some people prefer to film themselves while others use events around them as content.

Video Making Tools

Video Capturing Device

First, you will need a camera to capture video clips with. The high-end video cameras will cost you thousands of dollars. To start, however, you could choose to buy a low-end camcorder that allows you to take high-quality videos.

If you are creating a vlog or capturing videos outdoors, you may also use your smartphone mounted on a stabilising tripod or handheld stick. As soon as your videos improve; however, you may want to invest in a handheld or shoulder-top camcorder.

Microphone

Most video recording devices already come with a built-in microphone. However, if you are creating videos with a narrated audio, you may want a microphone that will make your audio sound clearer.

To start, you may use the audio recorder in your smartphone. However, you will need to do your recording in a quiet place to make sure that it does not pick up the unnecessary white noise.

Audio and Video Editing Software

Once you have your raw video footage and audio files, you will need editing software to put them together. If you have a separate audio file to edit, you may need an audio editor to improve its quality. Some of the things that you may need to do are to remove any background noise and to improve the pitch of your voice. For these simple tasks, you can make use of free audio editing software Audacity. While it is free, it is more than enough for most starting YouTubers.

Next, you will need a video editor. That type of software allows you to create a new video by putting together your raw audio and video files. Older versions of Microsoft Windows come with the Windows Movie Maker. While old, this software is excellent for beginners.

If you have your tools, all you must do is to practice in using them to create great videos. To find video editing styles, look at your favourite videos on YouTube and try to copy their transitions, timing, and other parts of the video.

Looking for a constant source of video content

The most daunting part of being a YouTuber is finding inspiration for new video content. Vloggers can upload videos every day because they only film themselves in their rooms talking in front of the camera. Even just doing this, however, still requires arduous work.

Most vloggers immediately start making their videos for the following day after creating their newest videos. Some channels post content weekly. By posting weekly, you will have more time to plan and create a video. One way to make the process easier is by creating a video post plan for an entire month. If you plan to post a video every week, you will need to prepare four videos and produce them at the same time. By planning your video's content, you will be able to avoid running out of video ideas to post.

Ideally, you want to stick to your niche when thinking of video ideas. The best YouTube channels talk about topics that other people are also interested in. If your channel talks about popular TV series, for example, make sure that you post videos regarding the most recent TV series. That will elevate the viewership of your videos.

In the end, you want to create videos on topics that you are also interested in. Jot down a list of the issues that you love and pick one channel topic from your list. You can rank the items in your inventory to decide which theme you are most passionate with.

With YouTube, you already have your work cut out for you when it comes to finding traffic. YouTube is like a social network. Millions of people are using the platform every day. It is just a matter of attracting them towards your videos.

Most of the traffic you will get will come through YouTube's own video suggestion system. As soon as a user goes into YouTube, he or she is shown multiple video suggestions. These suggestions vary per country. If the user is logged in, the recommendations will be tailored to fit his or her interests.

As an aspiring YouTuber, you need to understand how this process works. Here are some of the crucial details that you need to work on to make sure that your videos are suggested to the users:

Optimise the Text Content of your Videos

You will be getting an opportunity to add text components to your videos. These text components will be indexed by Google Search as well as the YouTube search algorithm. To increase the likelihood that your target audience will find your video, you want to include the right keywords in this part of your content.

You can add text contents in the title, description, and video tags. Make sure that you include related keywords in these sections of the video. In the title, you want to add a part that will hook the users. Here are some useful types of titles that you can use for your videos:

1. Ask a Question

   Many popular channels like TED Talks and TEDx Talks make use of questions to lure in audiences. For it to work, the question needs to be attractive to your target audience. Ideally, your video needs to have an answer to the problem. Otherwise, the users will feel disappointed with your video, and they may leave a "dislike" on it.

2. Mention a Famous Name

Many YouTube Users also go to the platform to look up information about their favourite public figure and celebrities. Politics, music, show business, and sports are all popular on the platform. If your video is in any way related to any celebrity, include their names in the title to give your video a boost.

3. Describe an event

If there is an exciting event that happens in the video, you can describe what happened and put that description in your title. That is the most commonly used form; however; it is useful in capturing the attention of YouTube users.

Optimising the description and the video tags

The description section and video tag allow you to add other keywords that may not have been included in your title. Only a small percentage of your users will check your video description. However, they are still an essential part of your content. For instance, this is the part where you could include links. You could use this section for your monetisation as well as for adding links to your sources.

The tags, on the other hand, are purely for the use of the YouTube ranking algorithm. You will need to add the most relevant keywords to these parts.

Use Engaging Thumbnails

Next to the title, YouTube users will look at your video thumbnail to learn what your video is about. Ideally, you want your thumbnails to work together with your title. It also works if you use engaging images in the thumbnail. People tend to be drawn towards images that they are already familiar with.

You could also use text and special symbols in your thumbnail to grab people's attention. In the past, people have used red arrows or red circles to make their thumbnails attract more attention.

Converting Traffic into Subscribers

Also, make it a habit to ask your viewers to subscribe to your channel. By subscribing and clicking on the bell button, the users will get a notification on their phones when you release a new video. To increase the chances of subscription, you could publish a video regularly and ask your users to subscribe and hit the bell button at the start of each video.

From Amateur to Professional

All that you have been doing until now is what any amateur would do. That chapter will turn you into a pro on YouTube. So, sit tight!

Make those thumbnails pop

A thumbnail refers to the small picture shown when your videos come up in a search result or are listed anywhere on YouTube's website. It may prove a random point from the video, or it can be a picture you upload that has words describing more of what happens. If you look at a few of the most admired channels on YouTube, both individual and professional, you will notice that most of the top channels have exceptionally clean and professional quality thumbnails.

While you may not want to spend all the time, it can take to create an impressive looking thumbnail. It should be noted how important it is to get many views on any video. Other than the video title, the thumbnail that represents your video is the first thing people see as soon as your video shows up in a search result or the recommended videos section. The quality, or lack of it, can make or break whether someone clicks on the video to view it.

To make great thumbnails:

1. Design it in unison with your title in such a way that will make users feel they have to view your video because it contains something amazing or unique.
2. Make the font of the words you put on the thumbnail look clean and modern.
3. Make the words you use on the thumbnail provocative and exciting.
4. Use a picture of high quality; a high definition shot in good focus that users will understand easily on any device.
5. Do not use Microsoft Paint to create their thumbnails. Use Canva or some other professional picture editing tool.

Annotations for calling your audience to action are those little pop-ups that come up while they are watching the video. These can lead to a higher number of subscribers by including them to click the popup while they watch your video.

Many video creators on YouTube noticed increased subscriptions to their channel when they added these. You can put in a link that encourages audience members to subscribe, or you can use a graphic. If you do this in a way that is not annoying or obnoxious, your subscriptions will grow as a result. However, if you annoyingly do this, you might lose potential subscribers.

Allow People to Discover you

YouTube gives users the choice to click a link and get sent to your website. So, if you already have a website, do this as soon as possible. There is utterly no reason not to take advantage of this option if you can. Any effort you dedicate to bringing video views to your channel can be taken advantage of any time you direct viewers to your webpage.

Besides, this will make your channel a verified, authentic source for your personal brand. In your YouTube page channel settings, you can add your blog URL or website to the channel. You could also add your URL or website to the description of your YouTube channel. You can also add a subscribe option button on your webpage or blog to bring more subscribers to your channel.

Intros and Outros

The intros and outros you use for YouTube will aid you in branding your name and will help your videos have a higher entertainment value. It will give your videos a professional feel and can be used as an opening theme, like a show that people come back to and enjoy the familiarity of. In addition to this, an appealing intro ensures your audience is more involved with your videos.

Be a Ruthless Editor

To get the best of your content out on the web, you must make a lot of it, and edit it ruthlessly. Most creative geniuses make a lot more content than they show, and what we see is their best work. It should apply to your YouTube videos too. Edit them fearlessly to ensure that you are only publishing your absolute best videos.

When you try to force yourself to publish on a strict schedule without taking the time to make the videos enjoyable, your brand will be hurt down the road. Make plenty of recordings for your final cut, but only publish the best. If you are unsure of a specific take, you can always take multiple shots. If you are using Windows, Adobe Premier is an excellent program for editing your videos.

Optimising Descriptions in your Videos

Returning to the SEO (search engine optimisation) side of making YouTube content, you should never neglect the description of your videos. Your video description will allow your content to be easily discovered in a search engine while also giving your potential audience members a sneak preview of what your content discusses. However, this should not be overdone.

Putting a detailed description in your video will not make any sense because the first few sentences are the only parts that are displayed when someone loads the video. Like your video title, the keyword should be used in the video description but not overdone. You cannot outsmart search engines by entering the keyword 20 times, which will just hurt your odds of getting displayed on search engines. Instead, make it authentic and natural.

You can put Google's Keyword Planner to productive use by finding relevant ideas to use for keywords in your videos, then adding them to your content and videos. That will allow you to be easier to discover on both YouTube and Google searches. If you overdo this, it is not going to help (and will do the opposite) but adding in some well-placed and researched words will help your rankings a lot.

Be mindful that if you have a low view count on your videos, it does not always mean your content is not good. It might just say that it is not easy to discover for viewers. Metadata plays a bit role in allowing your content to be more easily displayed to those who are searching. Look at some videos that are well-converting and look at the meta tags they have on them to get an idea of what works. However, do not simply copy/paste these tags because that will not work.

Think about How you End them

No matter what your video content is about, you should always end videos on a high note. Like the very last bit of dialogue before a play ends, videos should end in a way that is memorable and positive. Ask the viewers watching to subscribe and like your video if they enjoyed it, and then ask them to visit your blog our website. Keep in mind that if you do not ask for anything, you will not get anything.

End all your content with a confident flourish, allowing viewers to know you appreciate them. End videos in a positive way, smiling and leaving your audience eager to see more content from you.

Think about Collaboration

You can collaborate with other video creators on YouTube. It has turned into quite a common act among video makers. Why is that? Because when you work, everyone benefits from it. Your audience benefits, the people involved in the collaboration benefit, and so do you.

Creativity is all about being constructive and viewing other video creators as your competition does not help. Instead, celebrate the success of others and see how you can join to improve each other's success. Look for successful video creators in your field and see if you can collaborate to do an exciting project. And always remember to look for what you can add to their channel as well.

It will let you connect with new audience members that you may have never reached before. The person you collaborate with will also have access to new viewers. The audience will appreciate the new value and extra content, as well. As you can see, this is an advantage for all parties involved.

Make sure you Interact with Viewers

The art of social media relies on interaction and connection with people who share your common goals and ideas. It means that the amount you care directly influences your success. When the people viewing your content can tell you care for them as people, they will return the favour. No one wants to be involved with someone who does not care about them, even when they are just YouTube subscribers. Try to interact with your viewers, paying attention to the requests they give you in comments.

You might get some anger or backslash in comments, but do not allow that to distract you from paying attention to your loyal listeners and viewers. When your viewers take the time to comment on your videos, try to respond to what they are saying. That will build more trust between you and your audience, leading them to respect you for taking the time to connect. That is how you make a loyal fan base.

Do Challenges and Offer Price

Who does not like to receive prizes or complete challenges? After you build up a loyal fan base, you can offer them compensation for staying true to your channel. A contest r prize giveaway can help you to lure in new viewers and reward those who have stood by your channel. You can give away T-shirts, a tech gadget, or a free hosting subscription. The possibilities are endless.

No matter what you choose to give away, your viewers will appreciate receiving something free and will share this with their friends. That will give you an opportunity for free promotion, but also a possibility of viral advertising for your YouTube channel. For huge giveaways, some hosts on YouTube require that their audience members must subscribe to each of their social media platforms before they can enter the giveaway, which is a great approach. The prize items should be relevant to the niche of your videos, but it is okay even if they are not.

Promoting Across Platforms is a Must

In our modern social media age, being active and present across different platforms of social media is necessary for succeeding and growing any online audience. When you are attempting to create a brand for yourself, you must be discoverable. That means being active on more than one platform for social media. Try putting up profiles on Twitter and Facebook. However, you can go further and put up Instagram and SnapChat accounts too. You can give Google and Facebook ads a try to provide yourself with further promotion.

When you are visible throughout various platform online, you are making yourself far more apparent. Make sure that you are being aggressive about securing your first followers, which will, in turn, motivate you to create better content. You cannot just build a great website and expect your customers to show up right away. Use every resource you can to build up your brand. You can also share your channel with interested friends but try not to hassle or annoy them.

Keep on Trying

Experimenting and changing your methods until you find what works is the best approach anyone can take. Remember that there is never one single path to success and that what works for others might not always work best for your pursuits. Find what works for your brand and channel. That could include switching up the thumbnail, backgrounds, camera angles, and other techniques given to you in this chapter. Pay attention to the way your audience changes according to these changes, and always stay true to what your brand is about.

Making something memorable and valuable on YouTube will require lots of perseverance, time, effort, and dedication from you. However, if you stick with it and stay patient, it can work for you. These are only guidelines to get you started. Do not be scared to think creatively and come up with your methods!

Smart Ways to Beat Your Competition

If you want to use YouTube for company business, you must provide suggestions to your viewers. The fundamental way to use YouTube is just to do video clips that sell your product or service and solutions. That has better than nothing but as more of your opponent's use YouTube, just throwing video clips will not be enough run.

As more and more companies' business come onto YouTube, you need to provide more value to the industry for you to endure and flourish in your industry. The best way to stand out from your opponent is to give guidelines through your video clips regularly. That is because the majority of beginner YouTube promoters will only be concentrated on promoting their items and solutions. All their video clips will be about going to this website, blog or call this number or buy this or buy that. After a while, individuals will be fed up with that.

Provide valuable content

If you want to win in the YouTube activity for the long run, then you have to provide helpful information. Whether it is one video a week or one video every few days or even one video a day concentrated on discussing, at least one tip to your viewers that will make a tremendous effect on your company business actually, run. Not only will you get more brings and customers by doing that, but you will start to separate yourself from all the other YouTube promoters who are capturing themselves on foot by looking like anxious sales representatives looking for some fast cash. So, provide value regularly, and you will win the audience.

Use Power of Face to Face Human Touch

One of the most frustrating things I come across is video clips where the individual never reveals their face. Some individuals have YouTube programs where they display their items or discuss their solutions but never show their face. Do you know what that does to your audience?

You viewers can gradually get frustrated with you and incorrect with you!

What are you trying to hide? Why are you trying to cover something? Is something incorrect with you, or do you have some unsure business? If you want to use YouTube for your company business and build the highest possible achievements, then you have to set it off and be willing to display the experience.

Showing the experience will make a considerable improvement in your company business. Individuals usually like, link, and believe in you even more. Your company business will experience more individual to them. The more they experience they know you, the more they will purchase from you. If you are an entrepreneur, then your advantage appears in that you can provide that personal touch to your clients while the big organisations cannot as much!

So, use that personal touch to your advantage by displaying the experience in your video clips.

To do that, do face to face videos! Face to experience video clips is video clips where you only need to display the experience as if you are discussing to them on a digital camera one-to-one — no more concealing the face any longer. That is poor, uncommitted and cowardly. Just display the face and go all the way. Then this will do amazing things for your company business.

Mix Up Your Videos

You can go to the best cafe in the world. Initially, you will love it, but if you go there over and over again, you will become ill of it. Similarly, your viewers will like to see a wide range in your video clips. So, my tip is to mix up your video clips. Do not always do the same type of video clips. Do not only educate guidelines in your video clips. Sometimes, show videos clip of you while you are on holiday having a fun time.

Do not always do videos clip clips where you are at the office. Do video clips while you are at the recreation area. Do video clips while you are by the seaside. Just mix it up. When you mix up your video clips, then it will be more fun to look at and give a little wider range to your viewers.

Follow The 80/20 Rule

When you do video clips, you should concentrate on following the 80% value to 20% message ratio. An increasing number of businesses are using YouTube to introduce themselves to the world. However, most of them are just throwing their video clips. They are essentially creating a bunch of "commercials" on YouTube. Now, that is better than nothing but let me ask you something. What do you do when an industrial comes on? You like to change the routeing channel.

In this mass confusion age, you have to go the one step further to stand out from your competition. To do that, you should to do less "pitch" video clips (a commercial type of videos) and concentrate on doing "value" video clips where you share tips, how-to tutorials, or any video that gives value to your viewers. As you provide more value to the marketplace, your income will soar because funds are just an exchange of value.

So, once you create your own YouTube route, do not just throw in video clips that offer massage video clips. Create 80% of your video clips of some value – whether it is a tutorial, an inspirational the message, a simple little tip, a lifestyle video, or something that can bring value to your viewers. Then 20% of the time, offer some message type of video where you sell them your products and services.

The goal of value video clips is to have the people like/trust/connect with you because whenever someone shares with you something, you start to believe in them more and want to learn more from them. The goal of these video clips is to earn cash. The key is to provide both value and message video clips to make some money from online video marketing.

Use Exclusive Videos for Subscribers

YouTube has a choice to unlisted videos clip so that the regular community cannot look for that video on YouTube Google. The only way to see that video is to have the YouTube web link. Do not just hand out everything for 100%. Make stages of content material. Free content material can be on your route channel. But once they are in your list record, you can deliver them even better unlisted and unique material.

Once they buy your items, they get even better personal content material as well.

Create Multiple YouTube Channel

Have an active channel and some supportive ones.

It is never excellent to put all your egg in one container. Broaden your container by developing multiple YouTube programs. One YouTube route channel can have 2 to 20 video clips. Then another YouTube the route can have to 2 to 12 video clips and so forth. That way, if one YouTube route channel goes down, then you have another set of YouTube program to yourself.

Use the Multi-Platform Video Strategy

If you are serious about using online video promotion, then apply several video systems platforms. Did you know that YouTube is not the only video system that positions well on Google?

There are other online video promotion systems that you can use that can position well on. Look for engine search engines. One is Dailymotion. The best part about DailyMotion is that they are not known to take down their content material creator's programs easily. They also perform great on search engines.

Another video system is Vimeo. Videos that are submitted on Vimeo seem to position well on Google if you do the right SEO to it. However, Vimeo is not very helpful to the people in the internet marketing/affiliate marketing/business chance market, so if that is your market, stay away from Vimeo.

Having video clips in different video systems (such as YouTube, Dailymotion, Vimeo), you open up the opportunity for all those three video clips hyperlinks to show and rank on Google.

Bonus Chapter: Tips to Nail Your Personal Branding

Creating a personal brand is not easy. It is not unusual to forget yourself in the process and reach nowhere. Even when you know where to begin, you can feel lost. That is okay. Nobody gets it right the first time. The key is never to stop trying. Work with what you have, assess the output, tweak the process and reassess. Iterations will gradually build your influence.

Here are ten fantastic tips that will help you create a genuinely engaging and influential personal brand:

1: Have a focus.

2: Be authentic.

3: Have a story to tell.

4: Stay consistent.

5: Accept failures.

6: Spread positivity.

7: Follow your idols.

8: Walk the talk.

9: Let people talk about you.

10: Create a legacy.

1. Have a focus.

You cannot please everyone. You can do everything or be someone to everyone. Make peace with that and maintain your focus on your key message because that is unique to you. Having a single focus will resonate with firmly with one target audience, which will make it easier for the audience to identify with you. That will also help you create better content around your personal brand.

Once you have carved you niche, carve one within it. Go deeper. Be specific. Become memorable.

2. Be authentic.

The easiest way to nail your personal brand is to be yourself. If you are finding that difficult, then perhaps you need to make peace with yourself first. You need to be at ease with who you are and what your flaws may be. People can see through drama and façade. You cannot dupe them into buying you without conveying how happy you are with yourself.

It will also make content creation easier. It will be a no-brainer. A little fine-tuning here and there and you are done. Faster turnaround time will ensure consistent content generation and engagement. But it begins with being genuine and authentic.

3. Have a story to tell.

Why? Because stories sell. Period.

An old pendant is just an old pendant worth penny. But if you say that the Queen gifted this pendant to her most loyal servant and midwife after the birth of her eldest son, suddenly, the pendant is worth millions. So, if you want to sell yourself better, you need to package your skills inside a beautiful; wrapping of a story.

Everyone has a story; the only catch is finding it. Founding your personal brand on your journey, on your story will make it unique and powerful. With a story by your side, you will no longer be boring or just someone in the sea of many. You will be a warm person who lived an authentic, extraordinary life.

4. Stay consistent.

Staying consistent and having a focus go hand in hand. If you consistently create content around one single topic, people start associating that topic with you, and you slowly become the voice for it. Having too many focus areas or not following through with your messaging or plan will confuse your audience increasing attrition and decreased engagement.

So, do not underestimate inconsistencies thinking that no one will notice them. When you are an influencer, people nibble on your content not just in comments, but in their chats and offline as well.

Even if your personal brand is fun, you can have a catchphrase at the end or a style of editing to maintain consistency. It sounds corporatish, but that is going to do wonders for you. Because corporates became huge for the same reason – they were consistent.

5. Accept failures.

It is easier said than done. It is human nature to avoid failure, and that makes us conservative. As an influencer, you need to be creative. So be ready to fail. Embrace it like a friend.

Trying new things and failing at some or all of them will give you a better understanding of your personal brand. Remember, we talked about iterations. Failures are those iterations that tell you what is working and what is not. Keep experimenting, fail fast, succeed faster.

6. Spread positivity.

Often, we hear news about celebrities who acted out in public or treated someone badly, and we instantly lose respect for them. We feel that success has gone to their heads and has turned them into arrogant snobs. However, we also hear cases of people who became humbler after tasting victory. Their stories inspire you to be better.

So, when you gain that influence and become famous, do not burn bridges with people or brands. Stay true to your personal brand and your values. Never forget to leave a positive impact on others regardless of what you are doing and where you are.

7. Follow your idols.

To learn the tricks of the trade, we look up to our idols. It not only helps us initially to set footing and distinguish right from wrong but also guides us later in management of projects and fame. Start noticing what they do and how they do it. Add your unique flavour to it and continue. They have a team of experts guiding them, but you do not. However, mimicking their mannerisms when you cannot figure out your own will slowly get you around.

8. Walk the talk.

While it seems natural to create two different profiles – one for your brand and other for your friends and family – things tend to get messy. Keeping two separate accounts is only a mechanical part. You can go ahead with that. However, even when you are interacting with your family and friends or are present on informal occasions, your personal brand follows you. You can be two different people at the same time.

So, walk your talk wherever you go to stay authentic to your brand promise and image.

9. Let people talk about you.

Always talking about yourself will make you seem like an attention seeker. So, encourage people to tag you, message you or share their views about you even when you do not agree with them. Let them tell your story.

In case you do not agree with them, give that story to your people and watch them turn it around for you. That is the best PR you can get where you will also get to know what people think of you and how they defend you. That is your community!

10. Create a legacy.

Your personal brand will live till you live. But can you make it live longer? What if you want to exit this business? What happens to your brand? Think about this right now.

Even when you are not creating content anymore or engaging in that topic, people are mentioning, tagging and pulling you into those conversations. That is your legacy. Your exit strategy. Think about what you can do now to make that happen.

Final Thoughts

As you may have understood by now, this book is populated with all of the secrets that you need to know to grow your clout on Instagram and YouTube in 2020 – whether you have been around on these platforms for a while or if you are starting this year!

We sincerely hope that by reading this book, you were able to discover plenty of great information about Instagram and YouTube and how you can encourage growth so that you no longer have to worry about creating content and delivering it to cricket. When you begin enforcing these strategies, your previously quiet or non-existent audience will start growing and will add spark to life, and you will start seeing significant growth on your influencer.

Even though these platforms are still new and evolving each day, they have several significant influencers. It might seem intimidating initially, but there is always an excellent opportunity for you to connect with your audience and grow a position of authority in your niche. Despite what rumours may lead you to believe, no niche is saturated, and there is still plenty to be gained from it.

Think of it this way: YouTube and Instagram earn money when people like you create an influential platform through them and use it to draw more attention to their platform. As you grow and start building a name for yourself, they will promote your content so that you and your audience can become even more on their platform. It not only leads to enormous growth for you but for themselves also.

By using the secrets in this very book, you can grow yourself to the point that YouTube and Instagram want to support your growth as well to ensure that you are both experiencing success from their platform. That shared investment in your growth means that no matter how old these platforms are, there will always be room for more influencers to step in and make a name for themselves.

After you read this book, I hope that you go ahead and begin building your personal brand using the strategies that you were able to learn from this material. Start by choosing your niche and creating particular high-quality videos that are relevant to your audience and their interests. Once you have made your content strategy, ensure that you properly execute it, so your content is more likely to be found by the right audience or the audience that is most likely to love them!

After you have done everything you could to leverage these two platforms through designing and SEO strategising, you will need to move over to other social media platforms. This way, you can start building a name for yourself around the web. That will not only deepen your relationship with your followers, but it will also give you several avenues to approach new viewers on for them to find you on YouTube. That way, you maximise your growth potential so that you receive the desirable number of viewers and the level of growth that you are aiming for.

Once your influence starts growing, you can begin taking advantage of monetisation features to earn you a more significant profit. Whether that includes direct marketing things to your audience, using advertisements, or using these platforms as a part of your sales funnel, make sure that your monetisation feature works best for you!

If you feel that you can logically do it, do not be afraid to leverage multiple monetisation features to gain maximum earnings through your investments. After you have mastered the process of growing your audience, all you need to do is continue to monitor your analytics and promote your growth! Through this, you will build the momentum on your profiles and achieve the ultimate level of growth through your strategies, making all of your efforts completely worth your while.

Billions of videos are being watched on YouTube every single day-name it-but that will not hinder you in doing your stuff. Just remember, you need to find what your niche is and improve or enhance it, and you have to come up with a solid marketing plan. And if you feel stuck, make use of the smart strategies shared in chapter 13 to leap past your competitors in no time. Once you have these things, you are on your way to generating great income online!

After reading all the strategies from this book, you are now equipped with all the tools you need to start doing whatever it is that you need to do to an exciting content!

Sign up for my newsletter by leaving us your email, you will be informed about new promotions and new book releases:

Click Here **https://mailchi.mp/e136f3ee924a/stephan-anderson**

Stephan Anderson

Made in the USA
Middletown, DE
31 December 2019